Interactive Notebooks

Kindergarten

Credits

Content Editor: Angela Triplett

Visit *carsondellosa.com* for correlations to Common Core, state, national, and Canadian provincial standards.

Carson-Dellosa Publishing, LLC
PO Box 35665
Greensboro, NC 27425 USA
carsondellosa.com

978-1-4838-2461-1
01-187157784

Table of Contents

What Are Interactive Notebooks? 3

Getting Started 4

What Type of Notebook Should I Use? 5

How to Organize an Interactive Notebook . . . 6

Planning for the Year 8

Managing Interactive Notebooks
in the Classroom 10

Interactive Notebook Grading Rubric 11

Counting and Cardinality

Number Words and Sets 0 to 5 12

Number Words and Sets 6 to 10 14

Counting Objects 1 to 5 16

Counting Objects 6 to 10 18

Number Order 1 to 10 20

Counting with Tally Marks. 22

Counting Sets to 20 24

Counting by Tens 26

Counting On 28

Comparing Sets 30

Comparing Numbers 1 to 10 32

Operations and Algebraic Thinking

Representing Addition and Subtraction . . .34

Addition Number Sentences. 36

Joining Sets 38

Related Addition Facts 0 to 5 40

Related Addition Facts 6 to 10. 42

Decomposing Numbers 44

Subtracting within 5. 46

Subtracting within 10 48

Addition and Subtraction Sentences 50

Solving Word Problems 52

Addition Word Problems 54

Subtraction Word Problems 56

Making Ten 58

Addition and Subtraction Facts 60

Number and Operations in Base Ten

A Ten and Some Ones 62

Measurement and Data

Comparing Objects by Length. 64

Comparing Objects by Size 66

Comparing Objects by Weight 68

Geometry

Positional Words 70

Two-Dimensional Shapes 72

Three-Dimensional Shapes 74

Analyzing Shapes 76

Reproducibles

Tabs 78

KWL Chart 79

Pockets 80

Shutter Folds 83

Flap Books and Flaps 85

Petal Folds 90

Accordian Folds. 92

Clamshell Fold 94

Puzzle Pieces 95

Flip Book 96

© Carson-Dellosa • CD-104645

What Are Interactive Notebooks?

Interactive notebooks are a unique form of note taking. Teachers guide students through creating pages of notes on new topics. Instead of being in the traditional linear, handwritten format, notes are colorful and spread across the pages. Notes also often include drawings, diagrams, and 3-D elements to make the material understandable and relevant. Students are encouraged to complete their notebook pages in ways that make sense to them. With this personalization, no two pages are exactly the same.

Because of their creative nature, interactive notebooks allow students to be active participants in their own learning. Teachers can easily differentiate pages to address the levels and needs of each learner. The notebooks are arranged sequentially, and students can create tables of contents as they create pages, making it simple for students to use their notebooks for reference throughout the year. The interactive, easily personalized format makes interactive notebooks ideal for engaging students in learning new concepts.

Using interactive notebooks can take as much or as little time as you like. Students will initially take longer to create pages but will get faster as they become familiar with the process of creating pages. You may choose to only create a notebook page as a class at the beginning of each unit, or you may choose to create a new page for each topic within a unit. You can decide what works best for your students and schedule.

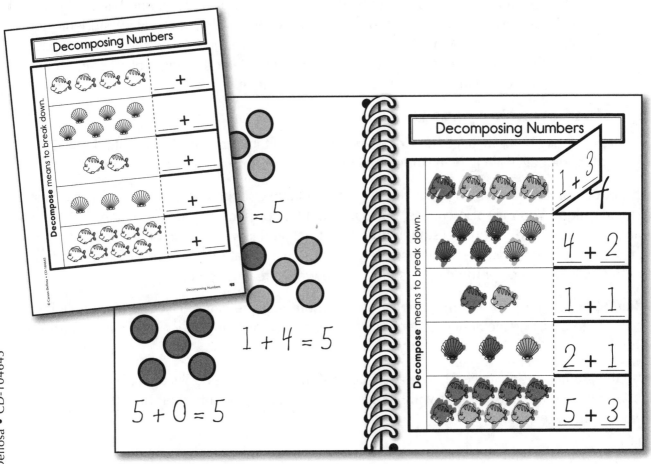

A student's interactive notebook for decomposing numbers

Getting Started

You can start using interactive notebooks at any point in the school year. Use the following guidelines to help you get started in your classroom. (For more specific details, management ideas, and tips, see page 10.)

1. Plan each notebook.

Use the planning template (page 9) to lay out a general plan for the topics you plan to cover in each notebook for the year.

2. Choose a notebook type.

Interactive notebooks are usually either single-subject, spiral-bound notebooks; composition books; or three-ring binders with loose-leaf paper. Each type presents pros and cons. See page 5 for a more in-depth look at each type of notebook.

3. Allow students to personalize their notebooks.

Have students decorate their notebook covers, as well as add their names and subjects. This provides a sense of ownership and emphasizes the personalized nature of the notebooks.

4. Number the pages and create the table of contents.

Have students number the bottom outside corner of each page, front and back. When completing a new page, adding a table of contents entry will be easy. Have students title the first page of each notebook "Table of Contents." Have them leave several blank pages at the front of each notebook for the table of contents. Refer to your general plan for an idea of about how many entries students will be creating.

5. Start creating pages.

Always begin a new page by adding an entry to the table of contents. Create the first notebook pages along with students to model proper format and expectations.

This book contains individual topics for you to introduce. Use the pages in the order that best fits your curriculum. You may also choose to alter the content presented to better match your school's curriculum. The provided lesson plans often do not instruct students to add color. Students should make their own choices about personalizing the content in ways that make sense to them. Encourage students to highlight and color the pages as they desire while creating them.

After introducing topics, you may choose to add more practice pages. Use the reproducibles (pages 78–96) to easily create new notebook pages for practice or to introduce topics not addressed in this book.

Use the grading rubric (page 11) to grade students' interactive notebooks at various points throughout the year. Provide students with copies of the rubric to glue into their notebooks and refer to as they create pages.

What Type of Notebook Should I Use?

Spiral Notebook

The pages in this book are formatted for a standard one-subject notebook.

Pros

- Notebook can be folded in half.
- Page size is larger.
- It is inexpensive.
- It often comes with pockets for storing materials.

Cons

- Pages can easily fall out.
- Spirals can snag or become misshapen.
- Page count and size vary widely.
- It is not as durable as a binder.

Tips

- Encase the spiral in duct tape to make it more durable.
- Keep the notebooks in a central place to prevent them from getting damaged in desks.

Composition Notebook

Pros

- Pages don't easily fall out.
- Page size and page count are standard.
- It is inexpensive.

Cons

- Notebook cannot be folded in half.
- Page size is smaller.
- It is not as durable as a binder.

Tips

- Copy pages meant for standard-sized notebooks at 85 or 90 percent. Test to see which works better for your notebook.

Binder with Loose-Leaf Paper

Pros

- Pages can be easily added, moved, or removed.
- Pages can be removed individually for grading.
- You can add full-page printed handouts.
- It has durable covers.

Cons

- Pages can easily fall out.
- Pages aren't durable.
- It is more expensive than a notebook.
- Students can easily misplace or lose pages.
- Larger size makes it more difficult to store.

Tips

- Provide hole reinforcers for damaged pages.

How to Organize an Interactive Notebook

You may organize an interactive notebook in many different ways. You may choose to organize it by unit and work sequentially through the book. Or, you may choose to create different sections that you will revisit and add to throughout the year. Choose the format that works best for your students and subject.

An interactive notebook includes different types of pages in addition to the pages students create. Non-content pages you may want to add include the following:

Title Page

This page is useful for quickly identifying notebooks. It is especially helpful in classrooms that use multiple interactive notebooks for different subjects. Have students write the subject (such as "Math") on the title page of each interactive notebook. They should also include their full names. You may choose to have them include other information such as the teacher's name, classroom number, or class period.

Table of Contents

The table of contents is an integral part of the interactive notebook. It makes referencing previously created pages quick and easy for students. Make sure that students leave several pages at the beginning of each notebook for a table of contents.

Expectations and Grading Rubric

It is helpful for each student to have a copy of the expectations for creating interactive notebook pages. You may choose to include a list of expectations for parents and students to sign, as well as a grading rubric (page 11).

Unit Title Pages

Consider using a single page at the beginning of each section to separate it. Title the page with the unit name. Add a tab (page 78) to the edge of the page to make it easy to flip to the unit. Add a table of contents for only the pages in that unit.

Glossary

Reserve a six-page section at the back of the notebook where students can create a glossary. Draw a line to split in half the front and back of each page, creating 24 sections. Combine Q and R and Y and Z to fit the entire alphabet. Have students add an entry as each new vocabulary word is introduced.

Formatting Student Notebook Pages

The other major consideration for planning an interactive notebook is how to treat the left and right sides of a notebook spread. Interactive journals are usually viewed with the notebook open flat. This creates a left side and a right side. You have several options for how to treat the two sides of the spread.

Traditionally, the right side is used for the teacher-directed part of the lesson, and the left side is used for students to interact with the lesson content. The lessons in this book use this format. However, you may prefer to switch the order for your class so that the teacher-directed learning is on the left and the student input is on the right.

It can also be important to include standards, learning objectives, or essential questions in interactive notebooks. You may choose to write these on the top-left side of each page before completing the teacher-directed page on the right side. You may also choose to have students include the "Introduction" part of each lesson in that same top-left section. This is the *in, through, out* method. Students enter *in* the lesson on the top left of the page, go *through* the lesson on the right page, and exit *out* of the lesson on the bottom left with a reflection activity.

The following chart details different types of items and activities that you could include on each side.

Left Side Student Output	Right Side Teacher-Directed Learning
• learning objectives • essential questions • I Can statements • brainstorming • making connections • summarizing • making conclusions • practice problems • opinions • questions • mnemonics • drawings and diagrams	• vocabulary and definitions • mini-lessons • folding activities • steps in a process • example problems • notes • diagrams • graphic organizers • hints and tips • big ideas

Planning for the Year

Making a general plan for interactive notebooks will help with planning, grading, and testing throughout the year. You do not need to plan every single page, but knowing what topics you will cover and in what order can be helpful in many ways.

Use the Interactive Notebook Plan (page 9) to plan your units and topics and where they should be placed in the notebooks. Remember to include enough pages at the beginning for the non-content pages, such as the title page, table of contents, and grading rubric. You may also want to leave a page at the beginning of each unit to place a mini table of contents for just that section.

In addition, when planning new pages, it can be helpful to sketch the pieces you will need to create. Use the following notebook template and notes to plan new pages.

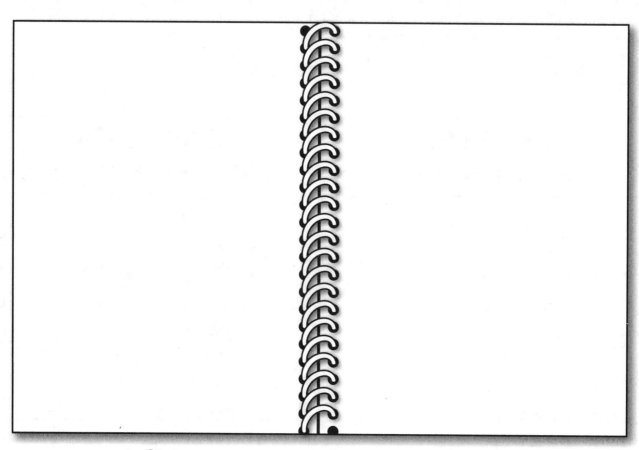

Left Side   **Right Side**

Notes

_____

_____

_____

8

Interactive Notebook Plan

Page	Topic	Page	Topic
1		51	
2		52	
3		53	
4		54	
5		55	
6		56	
7		57	
8		58	
9		59	
10		60	
11		61	
12		62	
13		63	
14		64	
15		65	
16		66	
17		67	
18		68	
19		69	
20		70	
21		71	
22		72	
23		73	
24		74	
25		75	
26		76	
27		77	
28		78	
29		79	
30		80	
31		81	
32		82	
33		83	
34		84	
35		85	
36		86	
37		87	
38		88	
39		89	
40		90	
41		91	
42		92	
43		93	
44		94	
45		95	
46		96	
47		97	
48		98	
49		99	
50		100	

Managing Interactive Notebooks in the Classroom

Working with Younger Students

- Use your yearly plan to preprogram a table of contents that you can copy and give to students to glue into their notebooks, instead of writing individual entries.

- Have assistants or parent volunteers precut pieces.

- Create glue sponges to make gluing easier. Place large sponges in plastic containers with white glue. The sponges will absorb the glue. Students can wipe the backs of pieces across the sponges to apply the glue with less mess.

Creating Notebook Pages

- For storing loose pieces, add a pocket to the inside back cover. Use the envelope pattern (page 81), an envelope, or a resealable plastic bag. Or, tape the bottom and side edges of the two last pages of the notebook together to create a large pocket.

- When writing under flaps, have students trace the outline of each flap so that they can visualize the writing boundary.

- Where the dashed line will be hidden on the inside of the fold, have students first fold the piece in the opposite direction so that they can see the dashed line. Then, students should fold the piece back the other way along the same fold line to create the fold in the correct direction.

- To avoid losing pieces, have students keep all of their scraps on their desks until they have finished each page.

- To contain paper scraps and avoid multiple trips to the trash can, provide small groups with small buckets or tubs.

- For students who run out of room, keep full and half sheets available. Students can glue these to the bottom of the pages and fold them up when not in use.

Dealing with Absences

- Create a model notebook for absent students to reference when they return to school.

- Have students cut a second set of pieces as they work on their own pages.

Using the Notebook

- To organize sections of the notebook, provide each student with a sheet of tabs (page 78).

- To easily find the next blank page, either cut off the top-right corner of each page as it is used or attach a long piece of yarn or ribbon to the back cover to be used as a bookmark.

Interactive Notebook Grading Rubric

4

_____ Table of contents is complete.

_____ All notebook pages are included.

_____ All notebook pages are complete.

_____ Notebook pages are neat and organized.

_____ Information is correct.

_____ Pages show personalization, evidence of learning, and original ideas.

3

_____ Table of contents is mostly complete.

_____ One notebook page is missing.

_____ Notebook pages are mostly complete.

_____ Notebook pages are mostly neat and organized.

_____ Information is mostly correct.

_____ Pages show some personalization, evidence of learning, and original ideas.

2

_____ Table of contents is missing a few entries.

_____ A few notebook pages are missing.

_____ A few notebook pages are incomplete.

_____ Notebook pages are somewhat messy and unorganized.

_____ Information has several errors.

_____ Pages show little personalization, evidence of learning, or original ideas.

1

_____ Table of contents is incomplete.

_____ Many notebook pages are missing.

_____ Many notebook pages are incomplete.

_____ Notebook pages are too messy and unorganized to use.

_____ Information is incorrect.

_____ Pages show no personalization, evidence of learning, or original ideas.

Number Words and Sets 0 to 5

Introduction

Read a picture book about counting numbers. Discuss the number words in the text. Write the number 1 on the board. Write the number word *one* below it. Ask students if they think the two mean the same thing. Have a volunteer come to the board and draw one object. Explain that a number represents an amount and that these are three ways to express the number 1 or the amount of 1. Continue introducing the other numbers 0 to 5 in the same manner. Discuss why the number 0 does not have a set of objects.

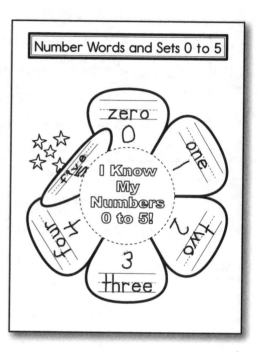

Creating the Notebook Page

Guide students through the following steps to complete the right-hand page in their notebooks.

1. Add a Table of Contents entry for the Number Words and Sets 0 to 5 pages.

2. Cut out the title and glue it to the top of the page.

3. Cut out the flower piece. Cut on the solid lines to create six petal-shaped flaps. Apply glue to the back of the center section and attach it to the page.

4. Count the numbers aloud, beginning with zero. Then, trace each number and the number word.

5. Draw a set of objects under each flap to represent the number.

Reflect on Learning

To complete the left-hand page, have students write each number word and number. Then, have students trace the number word and number three times each with different colors creating a rainbow effect.

Number Words and Sets 6 to 10

Introduction

Read a picture book about counting numbers. Discuss the number words in the text. Draw six objects on the board. As a class, count each object. Write the number word *six* under the objects. Have a volunteer come to the board and write the number 6. Explain that a number represents an amount and that these are three ways to express the number 6 or the amount of 6. Continue introducing the other numbers 7 to 10 in the same manner. Ask students what they notice about the number 10. A possible answer may be that it has two digits.

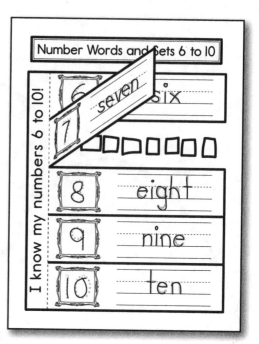

Creating the Notebook Page

Guide students through the following steps to complete the right-hand page in their notebooks.

1. Add a Table of Contents entry for the Number Words and Sets 6 to 10 pages.

2. Cut out the title and glue it to the top of the page.

3. Cut out the flap book. Cut on the solid lines to create five flaps. Apply glue to the back of the left section and attach it to the page.

4. Count the numbers aloud, beginning with six. Then, trace each number and the number word.

5. Draw a set of objects under each flap to represent the number.

Reflect on Learning

To complete the left-hand page, have students write each number word and number. Provide students with magazines and newspapers to find the number or number words *six* through *ten*. Have students glue them to the page next to the corresponding numbers.

14

I know my numbers 6 to 10!

six

seven

eight

nine

ten

Counting Objects 1 to 5

Introduction

Draw five baskets on the board. Number the baskets 1 to 5 in random order. Draw an apple in the basket marked 1. Ask students why only one apple is in the basket. Review how a number represents an amount. Have volunteers come to the board and draw the correct number of apples in the remaining baskets.

Creating the Notebook Page

Guide students through the following steps to complete the right-hand page in their notebooks.

1. Add a Table of Contents entry for the Counting Objects 1 to 5 pages.

2. Cut out the title and glue it to the top of the page.

3. Cut out the chef flap. Apply glue to the back of the top section and attach it to the page.

4. Cut out the pie cards. Count the number of pies on each card. Match each pie card to the correct number and glue the card on the gray glue space.

5. Draw a set of objects under each flap. Then, write the correct number to represent each set.

Reflect on Learning

To complete the left-hand page, have students draw five circles or "pizzas." Students should write a number 1 to 5 below each pizza. Then, have students draw a corresponding number of toppings on each pizza. For example, a pizza with the number 5 below it may have five slices of pepperoni drawn on it. Allow time for students to share their work.

Counting Objects I to 5

I can count objects up to 5!

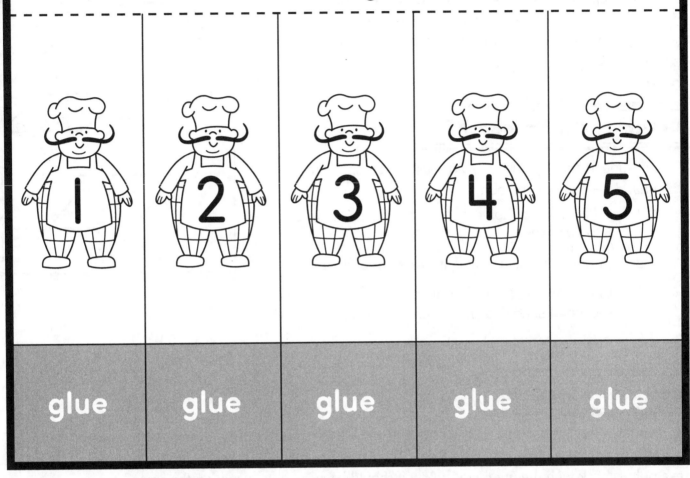

glue	glue	glue	glue	glue

Counting Objects 6 to 10

Introduction

Write the numbers 6 to 10 on separate index cards. Give the cards to five students or groups of students. Have them collect sets of objects to represent their numbers. For example, 6 pencils, 7 pieces of paper, 8 books, 9 markers, or 10 crayons. Have students bring their objects to the front of the room. As a class, count the objects aloud to see if the correct numbers were collected.

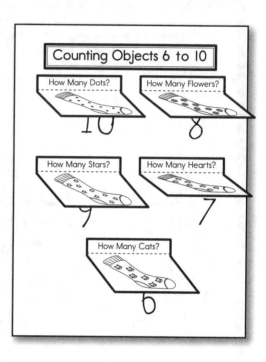

Creating the Notebook Page

Guide students through the following steps to complete the right-hand page in their notebooks.

1. Add a Table of Contents entry for the Counting Objects 6 to 10 pages.

2. Cut out the title and glue it to the top of the page.

3. Cut out the sock flaps. Apply glue to the back of the top section of each flap and attach it to the page.

4. Count the objects on each sock. Write the number under each flap.

Reflect on Learning

To complete the left-hand page, have students draw five socks. Students should write a number 6 to 10 below each sock. Then, have students draw a corresponding number of dots on each sock. For example, a sock with the number 6 below it should have six dots drawn on the sock.

Counting Objects 6 to 10

How Many Dots?

How Many Flowers?

How Many Stars?

How Many Hearts?

How Many Cats?

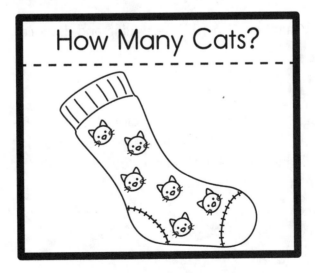

Number Order 1 to 10

Introduction

Display a number line 0 to 10. Ask students what they notice about the number line. Some possible answers may include that the number line begins at 0 or that it displays numbers in order. Have 10 volunteers stand at the front of the room. Beginning with the first student, count the number of students aloud, moving from one student to the next as you count. Explain that number order means a sequence of one number to the next (ascending order). Discuss how numbers can also be sequenced backward in descending order.

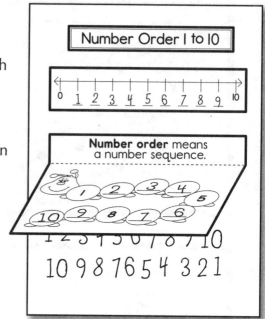

Creating the Notebook Page

Guide students through the following steps to complete the right-hand page in their notebooks.

1. Add a Table of Contents entry for the Number Order 1 to 10 pages.

2. Cut out the title and glue it to the top of the page.

3. Cut out the number line. Glue it below the title. Count along the number line and write each number as you count.

4. Cut out the caterpillar flap. Apply glue to the back of the top section and attach it below the number line.

5. Complete the number sequence on the caterpillar by writing the correct number in each blank.

6. Practice writing the numbers 1 to 10 in ascending and descending order under the flap.

Reflect on Learning

To complete the left-hand page, have students draw 10 blocks. Students should draw a dot in the first block and label it *1*, two dots in the second block and label it *2*, continuing the process until they have drawn 10 dots in the last block and labeled it *10*. Have students practice counting the dots aloud in ascending and descending order.

Number Order 1 to 10

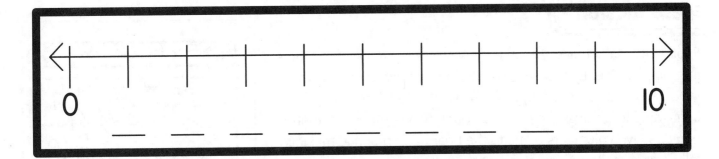

Number order means
a number sequence.

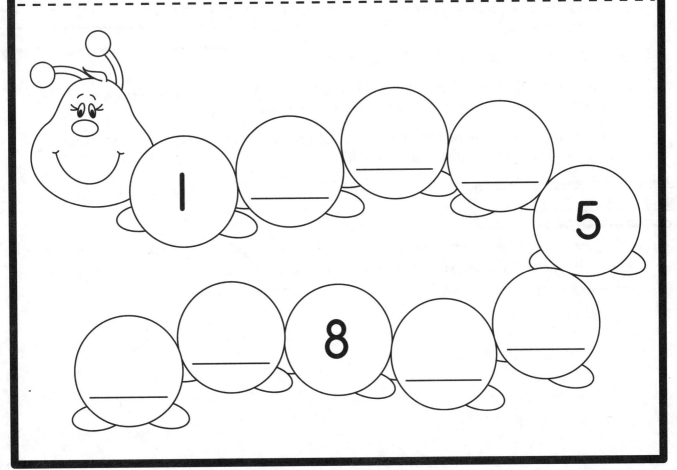

Counting with Tally Marks

Students will need five wooden craft sticks to complete the reflection activity.

Introduction

Explain that tally marks are an easy way to keep track of numbers in groups of five. Demonstrate on the board how to draw a line for each of the first four objects you count. Model how to draw a diagonal line across the previous four when you count the fifth object. Have volunteers come to the board and practice making tally marks as they count a given set of objects.

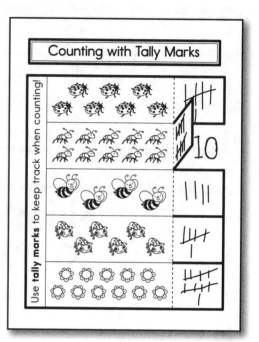

Creating the Notebook Page

Guide students through the following steps to complete the right-hand page in their notebooks.

1. Add a Table of Contents entry for the Counting with Tally Marks pages.

2. Cut out the title and glue it to the top of the page.

3. Cut out the flap book. Cut on the solid lines to create five short flaps. Apply glue to the back of the entire left section of the flap book and attach it to the page.

4. Count the objects beside each flap. Draw tally marks on the flap as you count. Then, write the number of tally marks under each flap.

Reflect on Learning

To complete the left-hand page, provide each student with five wooden craft sticks. Have students color and decorate the sticks. For example, the students can make the sticks look like people or animals. Then, have students glue the sticks on their page in a tally mark formation.

Counting with Tally Marks

Use tally **marks** to keep track when counting!

Counting Sets to 20

Introduction

Draw a set of five objects and a set of 20 objects on the board. Ask students which set would be the easiest to count and why. Ask students what strategies they can use to count a larger number of objects. Some possible answers may include using tally marks or circling groups of five or 10 objects.

Creating the Notebook Page

Guide students through the following steps to complete the right-hand page in their notebooks.

1. Add a Table of Contents entry for the Counting Sets to 20 pages.

2. Cut out the title and glue it to the top of the page.

3. Cut out the flap book. Cut on the solid lines to create four flaps on each side. Apply glue to the back of the center section and attach it to the page.

4. Count the objects on each flap using one of the strategies discussed in the introduction.

5. Write the number of objects in each set under the flap.

Reflect on Learning

To complete the left-hand page, provide students with magazines or newspapers. Have students look for groups of objects such as a basket of apples or a group of people. Have students cut out the pictures and glue them onto the page. Then, they should count the objects and write the number below each picture.

24

Counting Sets to 20

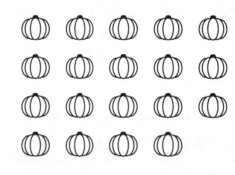

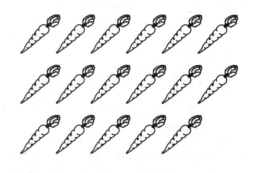

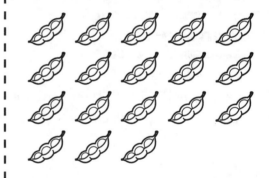

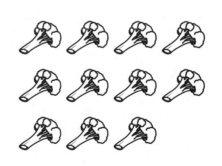

How many are in each set?

Counting by Tens

Introduction

Place 100 counters on a table. Ask students to help you count them aloud. Then, have volunteers come to the table and separate the counters into groups of 10. As a class, count the objects again by tens. Explain that counting a large number of objects by grouping them into sets of 10 is a faster way to count.

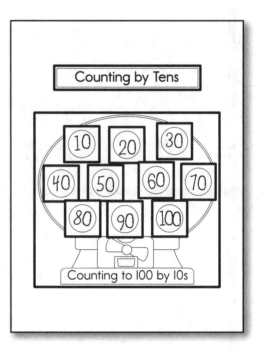

Creating the Notebook Page

Guide students through the following steps to complete the right-hand page in their notebooks.

1. Add a Table of Contents entry for the Counting by Tens pages.

2. Cut out the title and glue it to the top of the page.

3. Cut out the gum ball machine. Glue it to the center of the page.

4. Number the gum balls 10 to 100 by tens. Cut out the gum balls and glue them into the gum ball machine starting with 10 and ending with 100.

Reflect on Learning

To complete the left-hand page, have students draw 10 clouds. Students should count by tens and number the clouds 10 to 100. Then, have them draw 10 raindrops below each cloud. Students should pair with partners and practice counting by tens.

Counting by Tens

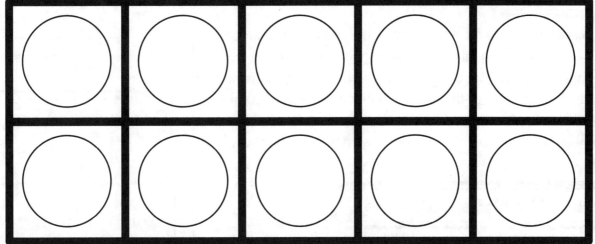

Counting to 100 by 10s

Counting On

Introduction

Have two volunteers stand at the front of the room. Ask students to count how many students are at the front of the room. Then, ask another student to join them. Again, ask how many students are standing at the front of the room. Continue this with several more students. Explain that each time you count on, you add one more to the group. Demonstrate how to use a number line when counting on from a number.

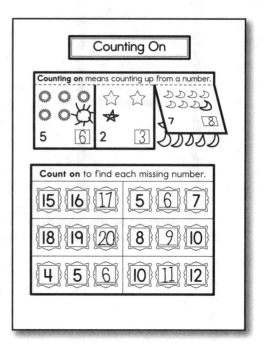

Creating the Notebook Page

Guide students through the following steps to complete the right-hand page in their notebooks.

1. Add a Table of Contents entry for the Counting On pages.

2. Cut out the title and glue it to the top of the page.

3. Cut out the flap book. Cut on the solid lines to create three flaps. Apply glue to the back of the top section and attach it to the page below the title.

4. Count the objects on each flap. Draw one more object in each set. Write the new number in the box. Draw a set with one more object under each flap.

5. Cut out the *Count on to find each missing number* piece. Glue it to the bottom of the page.

6. Complete each set of numbers by counting on. Write the number in the blank.

Reflect on Learning

To complete the left-hand page, have students create a "counting on" caterpillar. Have each student draw a circle for the head and face of the caterpillar near the top of the page. Then, have students draw another circle and write the number 2 inside. Students should add nine more circles for the body of the caterpillar, each time writing the next consecutive number in the circle. Allow time for students to share their work.

Counting On

Counting on means counting up from a number.

 5 ☐

  2 ☐

 7 ☐

Count on to find each missing number.

15	16	☐		5	☐	7
18	19	☐		8	☐	10
4	5	☐		10	☐	12

Comparing Sets

This lesson is designed to introduce one concept at a time and can be taught over several days.

Introduction

Discuss the terms *greater than, less than,* and *equal to.* Draw a group of five gum balls and a group of 10 gum balls on the board. Have a volunteer come to the board and circle the set that has the greater amount. Gather a group of four pencils and a group of nine pencils and place them on a desk. Have a volunteer pick up the group of pencils with the lesser amount. Finally, draw two equal sets of objects on the board. Have students count the number in each set. Discuss why the two sets are equal.

Creating the Notebook Page

Guide students through the following steps to complete the right-hand page in their notebooks.

1. Add a Table of Contents entry for the Comparing Sets pages.

2. Cut out the title and glue it to the top of the page.

3. Cut out the *Greater than means the larger amount* flap. Apply glue to the back of the title section and attach it below the title.

4. Count the objects in each set. Then, circle the set with the greater amount. Draw two different sets of objects under the flap. Circle the set with the greater amount of objects.

5. Repeat steps 3 and 4 with the *Less than means the smaller amount* flap, circling the sets with the lesser amounts.

6. Cut out the *Equal to means the same amount* flap. Apply glue to the back of the title section and attach it near the bottom of the page.

7. Count the objects on the left side of the flap. Then, circle the set on the right side of the flap that has the same amount. Draw two equal sets of objects under the flap.

Reflect on Learning

To complete the left-hand page, have each student draw a tree with three apples on it. Have students exchange notebooks with partners. Partners should draw apple trees that show more apples. Have students exchange notebooks again and then have partners draw apple trees that show fewer apples. Label the trees *more* and *less.*

Comparing Sets

Greater than means the **larger** amount.

Less than means the **smaller** amount.

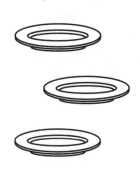

Equal to means the **same** amount.

Comparing Numbers 1 to 10

Students will need a sharpened pencil and a paper clip to complete the spinner activity.

Introduction

Explain the meaning of the word *compare*. Display a number line. Draw a *greater than* symbol on the board. Discuss the meaning of the words *greater* and *more*. Write the number 7 on the left-hand side of the symbol and the number 2 on the right-hand side. Using the number line, discuss how seven is more than or greater than two. Point out how the *greater than* symbol is always open to the larger number. Repeat the lesson using the *less than* symbol, pointing out how the *less than* symbol always points to the lesser number. Wrtie several pairs of numbers on the board. Have volunteers come to the board, compare the numbers, and write the correct symbol between each pair.

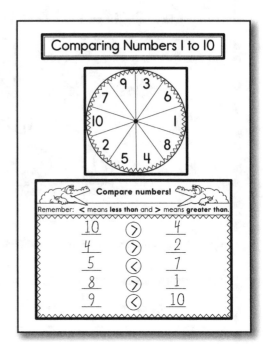

Creating the Notebook Page

Guide students through the following steps to complete the right-hand page in their notebooks.

1. Add a Table of Contents entry for the Comparing Numbers 1 to 10 pages.

2. Cut out the title and glue it to the top of the page.

3. Cut out the spinner. Glue it below the title.

4. Cut out the *Compare numbers!* chart and glue it below the spinner.

5. Use a sharpened pencil and a paper clip to spin the spinner. Write the number the spinner lands on in the first column. Spin again and write the number in the second column. If the same number is spun, spin again. Write the correct symbol to compare the numbers.

6. Repeat step 5 to complete the chart.

Reflect on Learning

To complete the left-hand page, provide students with magazines and newspapers. Have students cut out two groups of objects and glue them on the page, leaving space in between for a *greater than* or *less than* symbol. Students should count and write the number below each group. Then, students should write the correct comparison symbols.

© Carson-Dellosa • CD-104645

Comparing Numbers 1 to 10

Compare numbers!

Remember: **<** means **less than** and **>** means **greater than**.

_____ ◯ _____

_____ ◯ _____

_____ ◯ _____

_____ ◯ _____

_____ ◯ _____

Representing Addition and Subtraction

Demonstrate the various ways to represent addition and subtraction. Ask a volunteer to explain what one plus one is. Ask students to represent $1 + 1 = 2$ using their fingers. Then, ask them to clap it out. Have a volunteer come to the board and draw a representation of $1 + 1 = 2$ with objects. Have a volunteer come to the front of the room. Then, have another student join him. Explain that this is a way to act out a problem. Finally, write the number sentence on the board. Explain that there are many ways to represent addition. Repeat the activity using a subtraction sentence such as $2 - 1 = 1$.

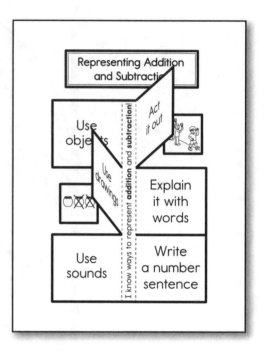

Creating the Notebook Page

Guide students through the following steps to complete the right-hand page in their notebooks.

1. Add a Table of Contents entry for the Representing Addition and Subtraction pages.

2. Cut out the title and glue it to the top of the page.

3. Cut out the flap book. Cut on the solid lines to create three flaps on each side. Apply glue to the back of the center section and attach it to the page.

4. Cut out the picture cards. Look at each picture and decide which representation is being used. Glue each card under the correct flap.

5. Use this page as a reference tool.

Reflect on Learning

To complete the left-hand page, write an addition problem and a subtraction problem on the board. Students should choose two ways to represent each problem and record their answers.

Representing Addition and Subtraction

Use
objects

Act
it out

Use
drawings

Explain
it with
words

Use
sounds

Write
a number
sentence

I know ways to represent **addition** and **subtraction**!

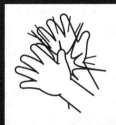

"I think
it means..."

2 – 1 = 1

Addition Number Sentences

Write 3 + 2 = 5 on the board and explain that a number sentence is a true statement about a group of numbers. Discuss the meanings of the addition symbol and the equal sign. Next, use a number line to visually explain the number sentence. Draw a number line 0 to 10 on the board. Draw an object such as a frog or rabbit above the number 3. Draw a line to show how it "hops" over two spaces on the number line. Discuss how the number sentence is related to the number line. Repeat this activity with several number sentences.

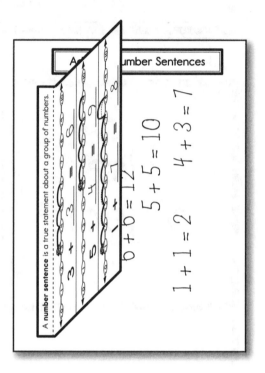

Creating the Notebook Page

Guide students through the following steps to complete the right-hand page in their notebooks.

1. Add a Table of Contents entry for the Addition Number Sentences pages.

2. Cut out the title and glue it to the top of the page.

3. Cut out the flap. Apply glue to the back of the title section and attach it vertically to the left side of the page.

4. For each number line, use a finger to start at the frog and "hop" or follow the dotted line. Count the number of hops. Write the number (addend) in the first blank. Complete the number sentence by writing the number that you landed on (sum).

5. Practice writing addition number sentences under the flap. Use the number line to help you find the sums.

Reflect on Learning

To complete the left-hand page, provide students with magazines and newspapers. Have them find and cut out two sets of objects and glue the sets side by side. Then, have them write number sentences to represent adding the two sets together. Encourage students to use the number line on the right-hand page to help find the sums.

Addition Number Sentences

A **number sentence** is a true statement about a group of numbers.

0 1 2 3 4 5 6 7 8 9 10

3 + ___ = ___

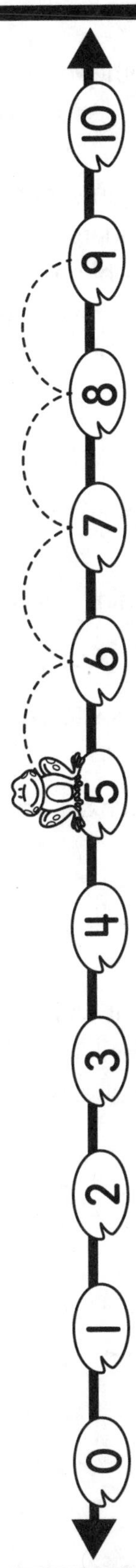

0 1 2 3 4 5 6 7 8 9 10

5 + ___ = ___

0 1 2 3 4 5 6 7 8 9 10

1 + ___ = ___

Joining Sets

Introduction

Explain the meaning of the word *join* as to put together or add to. Have three volunteers stand at the front of the room. As a class, count the number of students at the front of the room. Then, have two more volunteers join them. Ask how many students there are now. Write the number sentence 3 + 2 = 5 on the board. Circle the 5 and discuss how the answer to an addition problem is called the *sum*. Repeat the activity with a different number of volunteers each time.

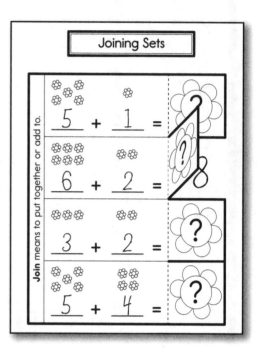

Creating the Notebook Page

Guide students through the following steps to complete the right-hand page in their notebooks.

1. Add a Table of Contents entry for the Joining Sets pages.

2. Cut out the title and glue it to the top of the page.

3. Cut out the flap book. Cut on the solid lines to create four short flaps. Apply glue to the entire left side of the book and attach it to the page.

4. For each section, count the flowers in each set and write the number. Add the two numbers and write the sum under the flap.

Reflect on Learning

To complete the left-hand page, provide each student with 10 two-sided counters. Each student should gather the counters in her hand and drop them on her desk. Then, she should count the set of yellow counters and the set of red counters and write a number sentence that represents the two sets. Finally, she should find the sum and record the answer.

Joining Sets

Join means to put together or add to.

🌸🌸🌸🌸🌸	🌸	**?**
_____ + _____		=
🌸🌸🌸🌸🌸🌸	🌸🌸	**?**
_____ + _____		=
🌸🌸🌸	🌸🌸	**?**
_____ + _____		=
🌸🌸🌸🌸	🌸🌸🌸🌸	**?**
_____ + _____		=

Related Addition Facts 0 to 5

Write the following related addition facts on the board: 0 + 4, 1 + 3, and 2 + 2. Ask students what they notice about the number sentences. A possible answer may be that the sum of all three is 4. Discuss how the numbers in the number sentences are different, but the sums are the same. Explain that numbers can be related like a family is related.

Creating the Notebook Page

Guide students through the following steps to complete the right-hand page in their notebooks.

1. Add a Table of Contents entry for the Related Addition Facts 0 to 5 pages.

2. Cut out the title and glue it to the top of the page.

3. Cut out the puzzle pieces.

4. Count the dots on each puzzle piece. Match each puzzle piece with the related addition fact.

5. When they are correctly matched, glue the puzzle pieces together on the page.

Reflect on Learning

To complete the left-hand page, have each student draw a house with three windows. Students should write a related addition fact for the number 2 (2 + 0, 0 + 2, 1 + 1) in each window.

Related Addition Facts 0 to 5

2 + 1

1 + 2

3 + 0

0 + 4

3 + 1

2 + 2

4 + 1

3 + 2

5 + 0

Related Addition Facts 0 to 5

4 + 1

3 + 1

2 + 2

0 + 4

1 + 2

3 + 0

2 + 1

3 + 2

5 + 0

Related Addition Facts 6 to 10

Introduction

Write the following related addition facts on the board: 2 + 4, 3 + 3, and 5 + 1. Ask students what they notice about the number sentences. A possible answer may be that the sum of all three is 6. Discuss how the numbers in the number sentences are different, but the sums are the same. Explain that numbers can be related like a family is related.

Creating the Notebook Page

Guide students through the following steps to complete the right-hand page in their notebooks.

1. Add a Table of Contents entry for the Related Addition Facts 6 to 10 pages.

2. Cut out the title and glue it to the top of the page.

3. Cut out the popcorn boxes. Glue two boxes on the top of the page and two boxes on the bottom of the page, leaving enough room to place the popcorn pieces on top of each box.

4. Cut out the popcorn pieces. Match each related addition fact to the correct number. Then, glue the popcorn piece above the popcorn box.

Reflect on Learning

To complete the left-hand page, have each student draw a popcorn box labeled *10* in the middle of his page. Write several addition facts on the board including three addition facts related to 10. Students should find the related addition facts for 10 and write them above their popcorn boxes.

Related Addition Facts 6 to 10

Decomposing Numbers

Discuss the meaning of the word *decompose*. Explain that a number can be broken down into parts to make the whole. Draw seven cubes on the board. Color five of the cubes green and color two of the cubes red. Ask students to give an addition sentence that would match the illustration on the board (5 + 2 = 7). Draw seven more cubes on the board. Have a volunteer decompose or break down the number 7 in a different way. Have another volunteer write the matching number sentence.

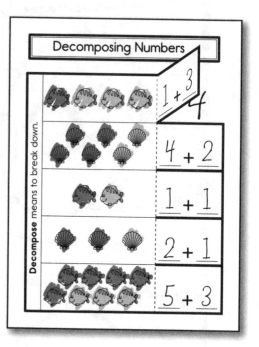

Creating the Notebook Page

Guide students through the following steps to complete the right-hand page in their notebooks.

1. Add a Table of Contents entry for the Decomposing Numbers pages.

2. Cut out the title and glue it to the top of the page.

3. Cut out the flap book. Cut on the solid lines to create five short flaps. Apply glue to the back of the entire left side of the book and attach it to the page.

4. For each section, use two different colors to shade in the objects. For example, on the first section you may color two fish blue and two fish red or one fish blue and three fish red.

5. Then, write a matching number sentence on the flap. For example, if one fish is blue and three fish are red, the matching number sentence would be 1 + 3.

6. Write the sum for the addition sentence under the flap.

Reflect on Learning

To complete the left-hand page, have students draw three sets of 5 circles. For each set of circles, students should color two different ways to represent the number 5 and then write an addition number sentence to represent each set of circles.

Decomposing Numbers

Decompose means to break down.

___ + ___

___ + ___

___ + ___

___ + ___

___ + ___

© Carson-Dellosa • CD-104645

Subtracting within 5

Introduction

Explain the meaning of the word *subtract* as to take apart or take from. Have five volunteers stand at the front of the room. As a class, count the students. Then, ask two of the students to return to their seats. Have students count the number of students who are still standing. Explain that they have just subtracted 2 from 5 and the answer is 3. Write a corresponding number sentence on the board. Draw four stars on the board. Cross out three stars. Ask students how many stars are left. Demonstrate on a number line how to subtract 3 from 4 by starting at 4 and "hopping" back 3 spaces. Write the number sentence 4 - 3 = 1.

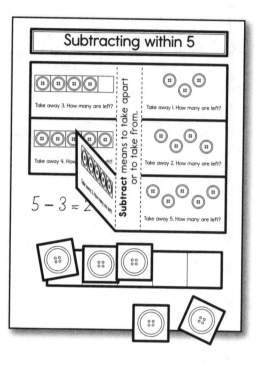

Creating the Notebook Page

Guide students through the following steps to complete the right-hand page in their notebooks.

1. Add a Table of Contents entry for the Subtracting within 5 pages.

2. Cut out the title and glue it to the top of the page.

3. Cut out the flap book. Cut on the solid lines to create three flaps on each side. Apply glue to the back of the center section and attach it below the title.

4. Cut out the five-frame piece and the 5 buttons. Glue the five-frame piece below the flap book. Use the five-frame and the button counters to solve the problems on the left side of the flap book. Then, read and follow the directions to cross off the buttons in each problem on the right side of the flap book.

5. Write a matching number sentence and the answer under each flap.

Reflect on Learning

To complete the left-hand page, write two subtraction problems within 5 on the board. Have students use the button counters from the right-hand page or manipulatives to solve the problems. Then, students should write number sentences to represent the problems.

Subtracting within 5

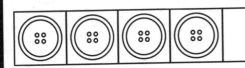

Take away 3. How many are left?

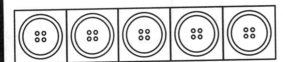

Take away 4. How many are left?

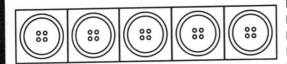

Take away 3. How many are left?

Subtract means to take apart or to take from.

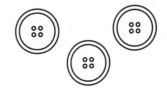

Take away 1. How many are left?

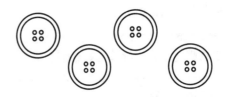

Take away 2. How many are left?

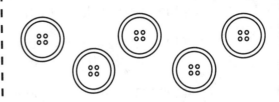

Take away 5. How many are left?

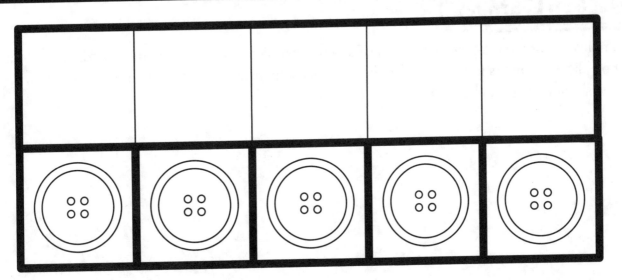

Subtracting within 10

Introduction

Review the meaning of the word *subtract* as to take apart or take from. Have eight volunteers stand at the front of the room. As a class, count the students. Then, ask three of the students to return to their seats. Have students count the number of students who are still standing. Explain that they have just subtracted 3 from 8, and the answer is 5. Write a corresponding number sentence on the board. Draw eight stars on the board. Cross out three of the stars. Ask students how many stars are left. Demonstrate on a number line how to subtract 3 from 8 by starting at 8 and "hopping" back 3 spaces. Write the number sentence 8 - 3 = 5.

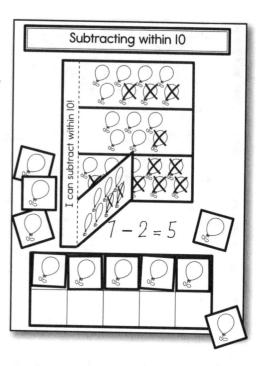

Creating the Notebook Page

Guide students through the following steps to complete the right-hand page in their notebooks.

1. Add a Table of Contents entry for the Subtracting within 10 pages.

2. Cut out the title and glue it to the top of the page.

3. Cut out the flap book. Cut on the solid lines to create four flaps. Apply glue to the back of the left section and attach it below the title.

4. Cut out the ten-frame piece and the 10 balloons. Glue the ten-frame piece below the flap book. For each flap, use the ten-frame piece and the balloons to help you solve the problem.

5. Write a matching number sentence and the answer under each flap.

Reflect on Learning

To complete the left-hand page, write two subtraction problems within 10 on the board. Have students use the balloon counters from the right-hand page or manipulatives to solve the problems. Then, students should write number sentences to represent the problems.

Subtracting within 10

I can subtract within 10!

Addition and Subtraction Sentences

Introduction

Review number sentences. Discuss the addition and subtraction symbols. Write an addition number sentence and a subtraction number sentence on the board. Circle the addition and subtraction symbol in each sentence. Explain that it is important to look at the symbol in the number sentence to determine if it is an addition or a subtraction problem. Then, have volunteers come to the board to solve each number sentence.

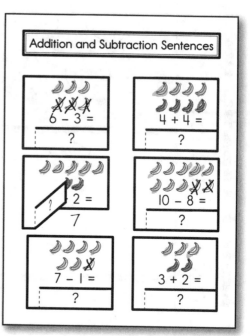

Creating the Notebook Page

Guide students through the following steps to complete the right-hand page in their notebooks.

1. Add a Table of Contents entry for the Addition and Subtraction Sentences pages.

2. Cut out the title and glue it to the top of the page.

3. Cut out the problem pieces. Cut on the solid line to create a flap at the bottom of each piece. Apply glue to the back of the left side and top section of each piece and attach it to the page.

4. Solve the problem on each piece and write the answer under the flap.

Reflect on Learning

To complete the left-hand page, provide each student with a photo or picture that includes several animals. Have students write one addition sentence and one subtraction sentence about the picture.

4 + 4 =

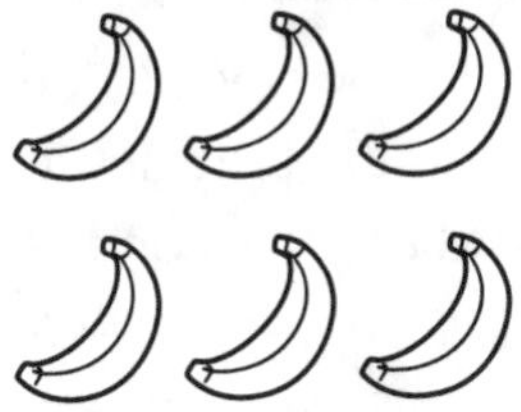

?

6 – 3 =

?

5 + 2 =

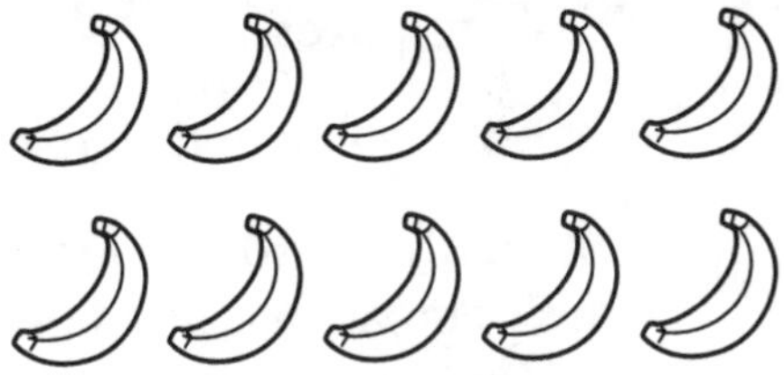

?

10 – 8 =

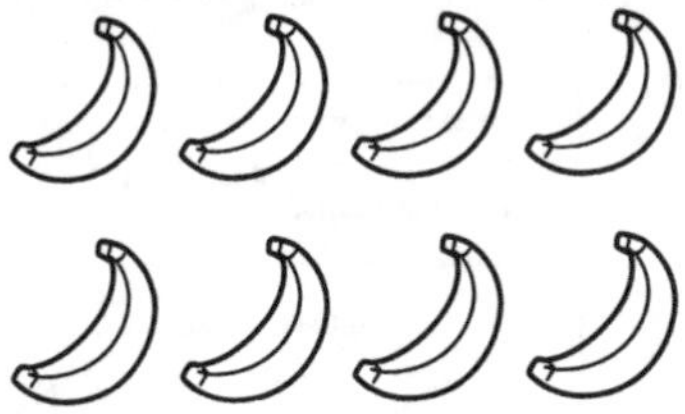

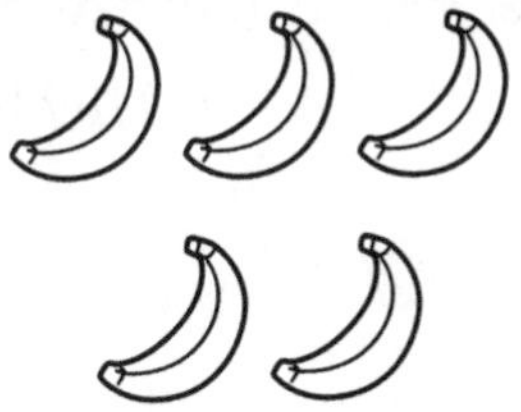

?

3 + 2 =

?

7 – 1 =

?

Solving Word Problems

Introduction

Review ways to use objects, fingers, drawings, equations, or acting out the situation as strategies to solving word problems. Write the following word problem on the board: *Jake has a sleepover on Friday night with 6 friends. In the morning, 4 friends go home. How many friends are still at Jake's house?* Have volunteers demonstrate which strategy they would use to solve the problem.

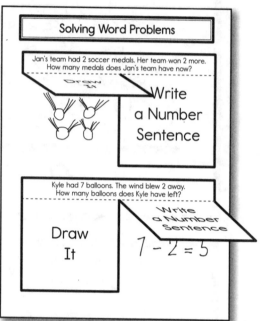

Creating the Notebook Page

Guide students through the following steps to complete the right-hand page in their notebooks.

1. Add a Table of Contents entry for the Solving Word Problems pages.

2. Cut out the title and glue it to the top of the page.

3. Cut out the word problem flap books. Cut on the solid lines to create two flaps on each one. Apply glue to the back of the top sections of each one and attach them to the page.

4. Read the word problem on each flap book. Under the left flap, draw a picture to solve the problem. Under the right flap, write a true number sentence.

Reflect on Learning

To complete the left-hand page, write the following word problem on the board: *Owen has 3 gum balls. His sister has 6 gum balls. How many gum balls do Owen and his sister have in all?* As a class, read the problem aloud. Provide students with access to manipulatives. Have students solve the problem using two different strategies and record the answers.

Solving Word Problems

Jan's team had 2 soccer medals. Her team won 2 more.
How many medals does Jan's team have now?

| Draw It | Write a Number Sentence |

Kyle had 7 balloons. The wind blew 2 away.
How many balloons does Kyle have left?

| Draw It | Write a Number Sentence |

Addition Word Problems

Introduction

Display a checklist of steps for solving a word problem. Review each step. Write the following word problem on the board: *Jose has 4 red crayons and 3 blue crayons. How many crayons does Jose have in all?* As a class, read the problem aloud. Have a volunteer come to the board, circle the numbers, and underline the question in the word problem. Have another volunteer come to the board and write a number sentence to solve the problem. Then, read the problem aloud again. Ask students if the answer makes sense.

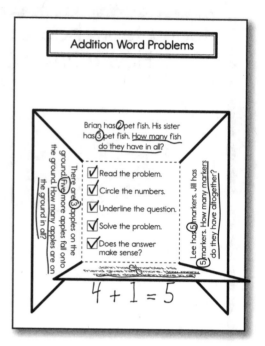

Creating the Notebook Page

Guide students through the following steps to complete the right-hand page in their notebooks.

1. Add a Table of Contents entry for the Addition Word Problems pages.

2. Cut out the title and glue it to the top of the page.

3. Cut out the word problem flap box. Cut on the solid lines to create four flaps. Apply glue to the back of the center section and attach it to the page.

4. Read the first word problem together. Then, read the checklist together to guide you through the problem. Use the checklist to solve the remaining word problems. Write a number sentence to solve the problem under each flap.

Reflect on Learning

To complete the left-hand page, write the following word problem on the board (or provide a copy for each student): *I have _____ pets. My friend has _____ pets. How many pets do we have in all?* Have students copy (or glue) the word problem in their notebooks. Students should fill in the first blank with the number of pets they own. Then, each student should ask a friend how many pets he has and record the number in the second blank. Finally, students should follow the checklist to solve the word problem and record the answer.

Addition Word Problems

Brian has 2 pet fish. His sister has 3 pet fish. How many fish do they have in all?

There are 3 apples on the ground. Five more apples fall onto the ground. How many apples are on the ground in all?

Lee has 5 markers. Jill has 5 markers. How many markers do they have altogether?

☐ Read the problem.

☐ Circle the numbers.

☐ Underline the question.

☐ Solve the problem.

☐ Does the answer make sense?

John has 4 marbles. His friend gives him 1 more. How many marbles does John have in all?

Subtraction Word Problems

Introduction

Display a checklist of steps for solving a word problem. Review each step. Write the following word problem on the board: *Emma had 6 bracelets for sale. She sold 4 of them. How many does she have left?* As a class, read the problem aloud. Have a volunteer come to the board, circle the numbers, and underline the question in the word problem. Have another volunteer come to the board and write a number sentence to solve the problem. Then, read the problem aloud again. Ask students if the answer makes sense.

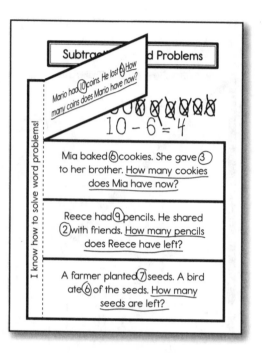

Creating the Notebook Page

Guide students through the following steps to complete the right-hand page in their notebooks.

1. Add a Table of Contents entry for the Subtraction Word Problems pages.

2. Cut out the title and glue it to the top of the page.

3. Cut out the flap book. Cut on the solid lines to create four flaps. Apply glue to the back of the left section and attach it to the page.

4. Read the first word problem together. Then, read the checklist together to guide you through the problem. Use the checklist to solve the remaining word problems. Write a number sentence to solve the problem under each flap.

Reflect on Learning

To complete the left-hand page, write the following word problem on the board (or provide a copy for each student): *I had _____ cookies. I shared _____ with my friend. How many cookies do I have left?* Have students copy (or glue) the word problem in their notebooks. Students should fill in the first blank with a number 6 to 10 and fill in the second blank with a number 1 to 5. Then, students should follow the checklist to solve the word problem and record the answer.

Subtraction Word Problems

Mario had 10 coins. He lost 6. How many coins does Mario have now?

Mia baked 6 cookies. She gave 3 to her brother. How many cookies does Mia have now?

Reece had 9 pencils. He shared 2 with friends. How many pencils does Reece have left?

A farmer planted 7 seeds. A bird ate 6 of the seeds. How many seeds are left?

Making Ten

Introduction

Have students brainstorm everything they know about the number 10. Write their responses on the board. Ask students to look for sets of 10 around the room. Have volunteers come to the board and write addition or subtraction sentences that include the number 10.

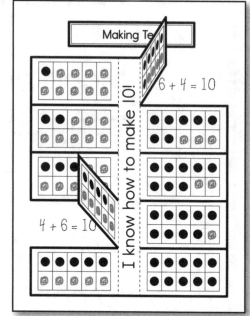

Creating the Notebook Page

Guide students through the following steps to complete the right-hand page in their notebooks.

1. Add a Table of Contents entry for the Making Ten pages.

2. Cut out the title and glue it to the top of the page.

3. Cut out the flap book. Cut on the solid lines to create five flaps on each side. Apply glue to the back of the center section and attach it to the page.

4. Look at the ten frame on each flap. Draw a dot in each empty space to fill the ten frame. Then, write a number sentence to represent the ten frame. For example, under the top-left flap, write 1 + 9 = 10. With a partner, discuss the patterns you see on or under the ten frames.

Reflect on Learning

To complete the left-hand page, draw the following pictures on the board: a slice of watermelon with 5 seeds, a gum ball machine with 3 gum balls inside, and a fishbowl with 6 fish. Have students copy the pictures from the board and draw objects on each picture to make ten. For example, students will draw the watermelon slice with 5 seeds and add 5 more seeds.

Making Ten

I know how to make 10!

Addition and Subtraction Facts

Introduction

Write the addition sentence 2 + 1 = 3 on the board. Have a volunteer come to the board and show one way to illustrate the equation. Erase the board. Ask students if there is a way to answer the equation 2 + 1 = 3 without counting. Discuss why it is helpful to remember addition and subtraction facts.

Creating the Notebook Page

Guide students through the following steps to complete the right-hand page in their notebooks.

1. Add a Table of Contents entry for the Addition and Subtraction Facts pages.

2. Cut out the title and glue it to the top of the page.

3. Cut out the crayon boxes. With the blank side faceup, apply glue to the bottom and side edges of each piece. Flip them over and attach them to the page to create two pockets.

4. Write the definitions for addition (*add* means to put together or add to) and subtraction (*subtract* means to take apart or take from) below each crayon box.

5. Cut out the crayon pieces. Read each fact. On the back of each one, write the answer. Use the cards to play a round of "crayon flash cards" with a partner. Store the cards in the correct addition or subtraction crayon box when finished.

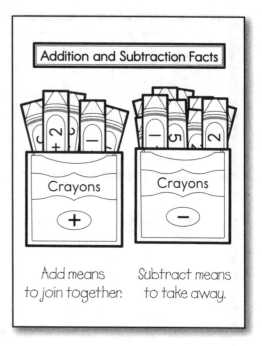

Reflect on Learning

To complete the left-hand page, have students draw five crayons. Then, students should write an addition or subtraction fact on each crayon. Have them exchange notebooks with partners and solve the problems.

Addition and Subtraction Facts

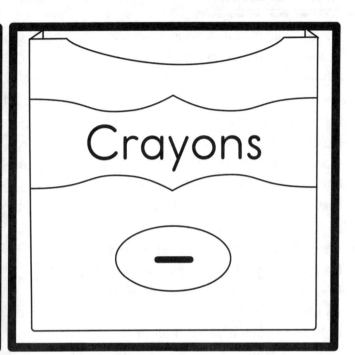

2 + 2	1 + 2
3 + 1	2 + 1
4 − 1	0 + 1
2 − 2	3 − 2
5 − 3	5 − 1

A Ten and Some Ones

Introduction

Have students count aloud from 0 to 20. Write the numbers on the board as the students count. Ask students if they notice anything different about the numbers as they counted past 10. Possible answers may include that there are two digits in each number or that each number begins with a 1. Draw 12 circles on the board. Color 10 of the circles. Explain that when counting larger numbers, grouping tens makes it easier to count. Ask students how many circles are left. Write *A ten and _____ ones is_____.* on the board. Have a volunteer fill in the blanks. Repeat the activity with several different numbers.

Creating the Notebook Page

Guide students through the following steps to complete the right-hand page in their notebooks.

1. Add a Table of Contents entry for the A Ten and Some Ones pages.

2. Cut out the title and glue it to the top of the page.

3. Cut out each problem piece. Fold on the dashed lines to create a trifold. Apply glue to the gray glue section of each piece and attach it to the page.

4. Count each set of dots. Then, color 10 dots. Write the number of dots left in the blank on the *10 + _____* flap.

5. Open each flap and write the total number of dots shown on the top flap.

Reflect on Learning

To complete the left-hand page, have students draw a set of objects (stars, triangles, hearts, etc.) up to 20. Then, students should circle the first 10 objects. Have students count the leftover objects and then write number sentences to represent their pictures.

62

A Ten and Some Ones

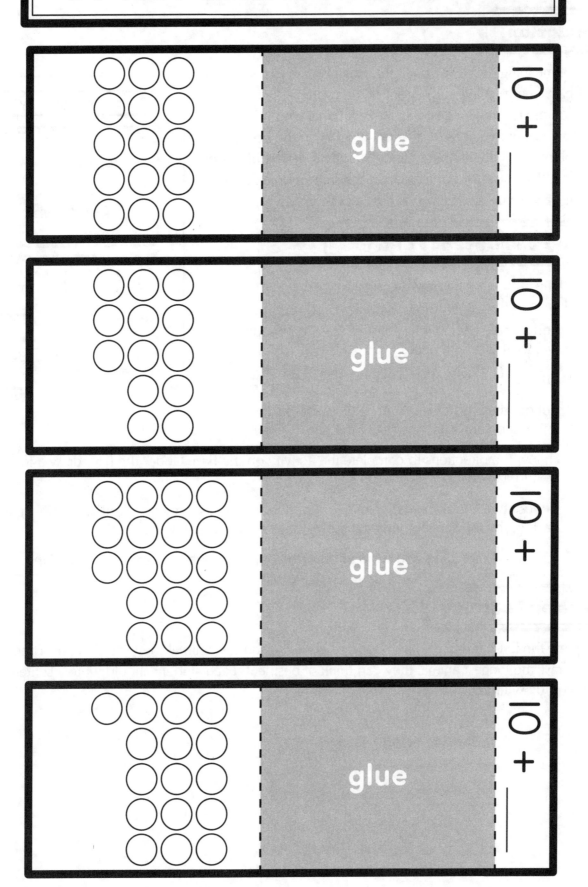

Comparing Objects by Length

Introduction

Explain the meaning of the word *length*. Have two volunteers with different hair lengths stand at the front of the room. Ask students which volunteer has the longest hair. Ask students who has the shortest hair. Draw two lines of different lengths on the board. Have a volunteer circle the longer line. Draw two more objects of different lengths. Have a volunteer circle the shorter object. Allow students time to share their observations about length.

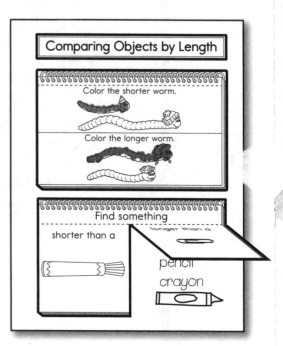

Creating the Notebook Page

Guide students through the following steps to complete the right-hand page in their notebooks.

1. Add a Table of Contents entry for the Comparing Objects by Length pages.

2. Cut out the title and glue it to the top of the page.

3. Cut out the worm flap. Apply glue to the back of the top section and attach it below the title.

4. Follow the directions to complete the activity on the flap. Under the flap, draw a long object next to a shorter object.

5. Cut out the *Find something* piece. Cut on the solid lines to create two flaps. Apply glue to the back of the top section and attach it to the bottom of the page.

6. Follow the directions and write or draw the object(s) found under the correct flap.

Reflect on Learning

To complete the left-hand page, have students draw the shortest animal they can think of. Then, have students draw the longest animal they can think of beside it. Each student should write a sentence about her picture. Allow time for students to share their work.

Comparing Objects by Length

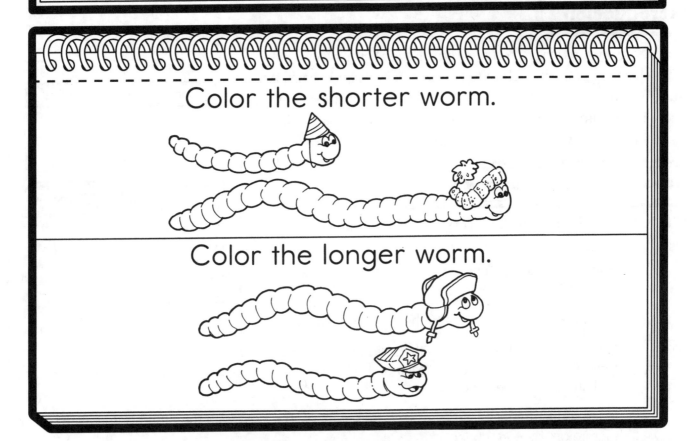

Color the shorter worm.

Color the longer worm.

Find something

| shorter than a | longer than a |

Comparing Objects by Size

Introduction

Read the story *Goldilocks and the Three Bears*. Discuss how the main character goes through different sizes of beds and chairs. Ask students why knowing the size of an object might be important. Then, have volunteers name the smallest and largest objects they can think of. Allow time to discuss students' answers.

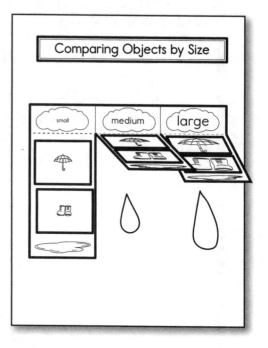

Creating the Notebook Page

Guide students through the following steps to complete the right-hand page in their notebooks.

1. Add a Table of Contents entry for the Comparing Objects by Size pages.

2. Cut out the title and glue it to the top of the page.

3. Cut out the flap book. Cut on the solid lines to create three flaps. Apply glue to the back of the top section and attach it to the page.

4. Cut out the picture cards. Compare the size of each object with the others. Glue each picture on the correct flap.

5. Draw a small raindrop, a medium raindrop, and a large raindrop under each corresponding flap.

Reflect on Learning

To complete the left-hand page, provide students with magazines and newspapers. Have students draw lines to create three columns labeled *Small, Medium,* and *Large*. Students should cut out pictures of objects that are different sizes and glue them into the correct columns. As an alternate activity, students can draw objects in each column.

Comparing Objects by Size

small	medium	large
glue	glue	glue
glue	glue	glue

Comparing Objects by Weight

Introduction

Explain the meaning of the word *weight*. Pass a book, such as a dictionary, around the class. Then, pass a lighter book around. Ask students which one is lighter and which one is heavier. Discuss how to determine the difference. A possible answer may be that the book that is heavier has more pages. Then, divide students into small groups. Give each group three objects. Students should arrange the objects from lightest to heaviest. Allow each group to explain how they determined how to arrange the objects.

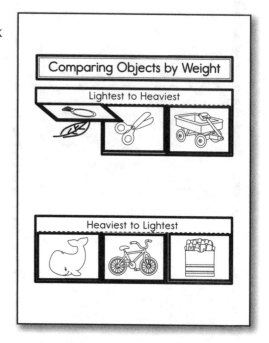

Creating the Notebook Page

Guide students through the following steps to complete the right-hand page in their notebooks.

1. Add a Table of Contents entry for the Comparing Objects by Weight pages.

2. Cut out the title and glue it to the top of the page.

3. Cut out the *Lightest to Heaviest* flap book. Cut on the solid lines to create three flaps. Apply glue to the back of the top section and attach it below the title.

4. Cut out the ring, wagon, and scissor picture cards. Glue each picture into the correct column from the lightest object to the heaviest object.

5. Draw three more objects from lightest to heaviest under each flap.

6. Cut out the *Heaviest to Lightest* flap book. Cut on the solid lines to create three flaps. Apply glue to the back of the top section and attach it to the bottom of the page.

7. Cut out the remaining picture cards. Glue each picture into the correct column from the heaviest object to the lightest object.

8. Draw three more objects from heaviest to lightest under each flap.

Reflect on Learning

To complete the left-hand page, have students find three objects in the classroom. Then, students should draw the objects in their notebooks from lightest to heaviest.

Comparing Objects by Weight

Lightest to Heaviest

glue	glue	glue

Heaviest to Lightest

glue	glue	glue

 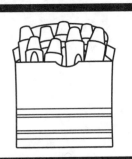 

Positional Words

Introduction

Explain that positional words tell where an object is in relation to another object. Have three volunteers stand in a line at the front of the room. Ask which student is *between* the others. Ask which student is *beside* another student. Then, play a game of I Spy with objects that are below, above, beside, in front of, or behind each other. For example say, "I spy something that is shaped like a rectangle above the door." The answer may be a flag.

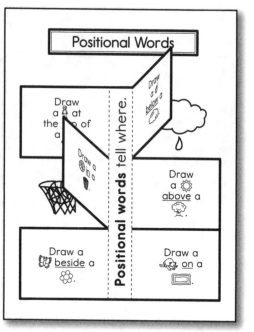

Creating the Notebook Page

Guide students through the following steps to complete the right-hand page in their notebooks.

1. Add a Table of Contents entry for the Positional Words pages.

2. Cut out the title and glue it to the top of the page.

3. Cut out the flap book. Cut on the solid lines to create three flaps on each side. Apply glue to the back of the center section and attach it to the page.

4. Read the sentence on each flap. Then, draw a picture that represents the sentence under each flap.

Reflect on Learning

To complete the left-hand page, write the following positional words on the board: *beside*, *in*, and *above*. Have students draw three boxes. Then, have each student draw a ball beside a box, in a box, and above a box. Finally, students should label the position of the ball in each drawing. Allow time for students to share their work.

Positional Words

Draw a 🧍 at the <u>top</u> of a 🛝.

Draw a 🏀 <u>in</u> a 🗑.

Draw a 🦋 <u>beside</u> a 🌼.

Positional words tell where.

Draw a 💧 <u>below</u> a ☁.

Draw a ☀ <u>above</u> a 🌳.

Draw a 🐱 <u>on</u> a 🔲.

Two-Dimensional Shapes

Introduction

Discuss the attributes (sides and corners) of circles, triangles, squares, rectangles and hexagons. Explain that flat shapes are sometimes called *two-dimensional* or *2-D shapes*. Give each student five self-stick notes. Students should draw each of the shapes on the self-stick notes. Then, have them find the five shapes around the classroom and label them with self-stick notes. Discuss how students determined which objects to label.

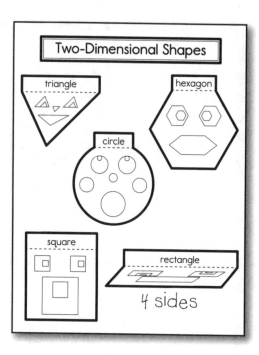

Creating the Notebook Page

Guide students through the following steps to complete the right-hand page in their notebooks.

1. Add a Table of Contents entry for the Two-Dimensional Shapes pages.

2. Cut out the title and glue it to the top of the page.

3. Cut out the shape flaps. Apply glue to the back of the top section of each shape and attach it to the page.

4. Write at least one attribute for the figure under the flap. (Answers may include triangle: 3 sides, hexagon: 6 sides, circle: no sides, square: 4 equal sides, or rectangle: 4 sides.)

Reflect on Learning

To complete the left-hand page, have students draw a picture of an animal using at least two of each shape. Write the following color key on the board: squares–green, rectangles–yellow, circles–red, triangles–blue, and hexagons–orange. Have students color the shapes in their animals with the correct colors. Allow time for students to share their work.

Two-Dimensional Shapes

triangle

hexagon

circle

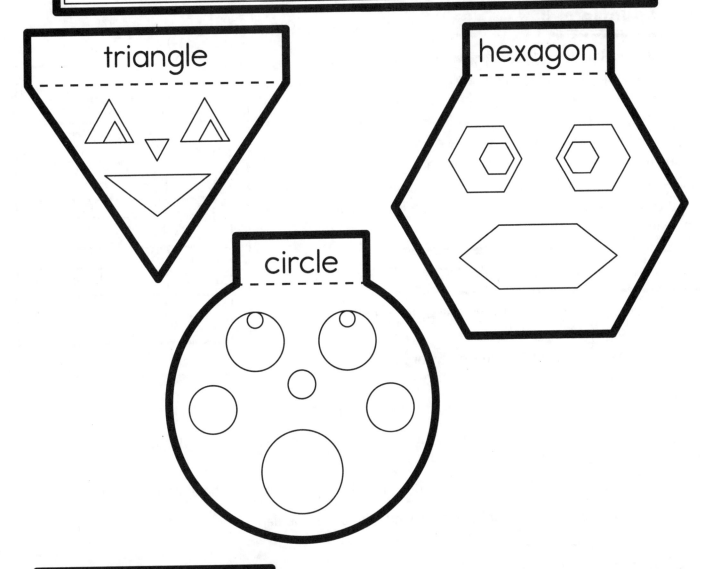

square

rectangle

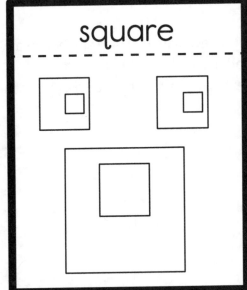

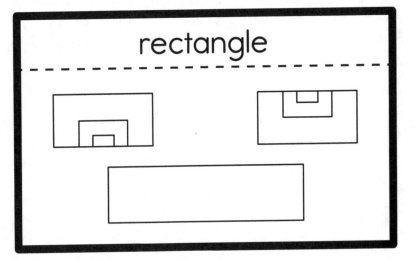

Three-Dimensional Shapes

Discuss the attributes (edges, faces, vertices) of cubes, cones, cylinders, and spheres. Explain that solid shapes are sometimes called *three-dimensional* or *3-D shapes*. Play a guessing game with self-stick notes. Draw a cone, a cylinder, a sphere, and a cube figure on four self-stick notes. Have a volunteer come to the front of the room. Attach one of the self-stick notes on his back. The other students should take turns providing clues about the figure so that the volunteer can guess which shape is on his back. Repeat the game with the other three shapes.

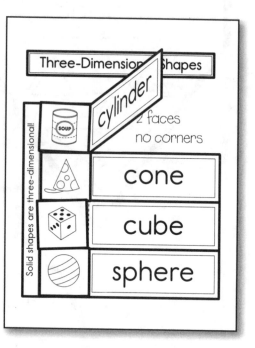

Creating the Notebook Page

Guide students through the following steps to complete the right-hand page in their notebooks.

1. Add a Table of Contents entry for the Three-Dimensional Shapes pages.

2. Cut out the title and glue it to the top of the page.

3. Cut out the flap book. Cut on the solid lines to create four flaps. Apply glue to the back of the left section and attach it to the page.

4. Cut out the four picture cards. Look at each shape. Glue each shape beside the correct flap.

5. Write at least two attributes for each figure under the flap.

Reflect on Learning

To complete the left-hand page, provide students with magazines and newspapers. Have students draw two lines to divide their pages into fourths. Then, students should label each box with the name of a solid shape. Students should cut out pictures of objects that represent each shape and glue them into the correct boxes.

74

Three-Dimensional Shapes

Solid shapes are three-dimensional!

glue	cylinder
glue	cone
glue	cube
glue	sphere

Analyzing Shapes

Discuss the differences between flat shapes and solid shapes. Display a large rubber ball and a flying disk. Ask students to tell you what they notice about each object. Demonstrate how a ball rolls freely on all sides while the disk will only roll on its edge. Then, display a self-stick note and a die. Have a volunteer tell you which shape is flat and which shape is solid. Challenge students to think of other real-world flat and solid shapes.

Creating the Notebook Page

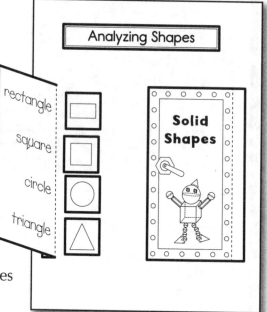

Guide students through the following steps to complete the right-hand page in their notebooks.

1. Add a Table of Contents entry for the Analyzing Shapes pages.

2. Cut out the title and glue it to the top of the page.

3. Cut out the shapes doors. Apply glue to the back of the narrow left and right side of each door. Attach them to the middle of the page, placing the pieces so that the insides of the doors align.

4. Cut out the shape cards. Look at each shape. Decide if the shape is solid or flat. Glue each shape in a column under the correct door.

5. Write the name of each shape on the inside door flap next to the shape.

Reflect on Learning

To complete the left-hand page, have each student draw a T-chart and label the two sides of the T-chart *Flat* and *Solid*. Have students draw a triangle, rectangle, circle, and square in the *Flat* column. Then, have students draw a real-world object that matches each flat shape in the *Solid* column. Allow time for students to share their work.

Analyzing Shapes

Flat Shapes

Solid Shapes

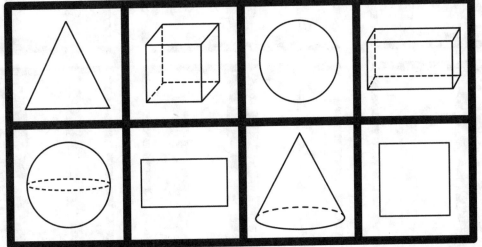

Tabs

Cut out each tab and label it. Apply glue to the back of each tab and align it on the outside edge of the page with only the label section showing beyond the edge. Then, fold each tab to seal the page inside.

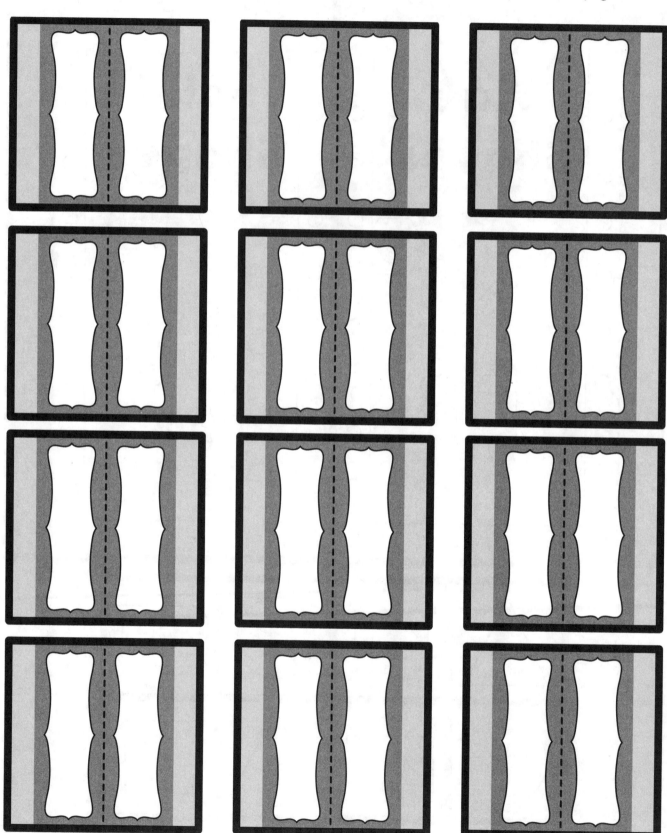

Cut out the KWL chart and cut on the solid lines to create three separate flaps. Apply glue to the back of the Topic section to attach the chart to a notebook page.

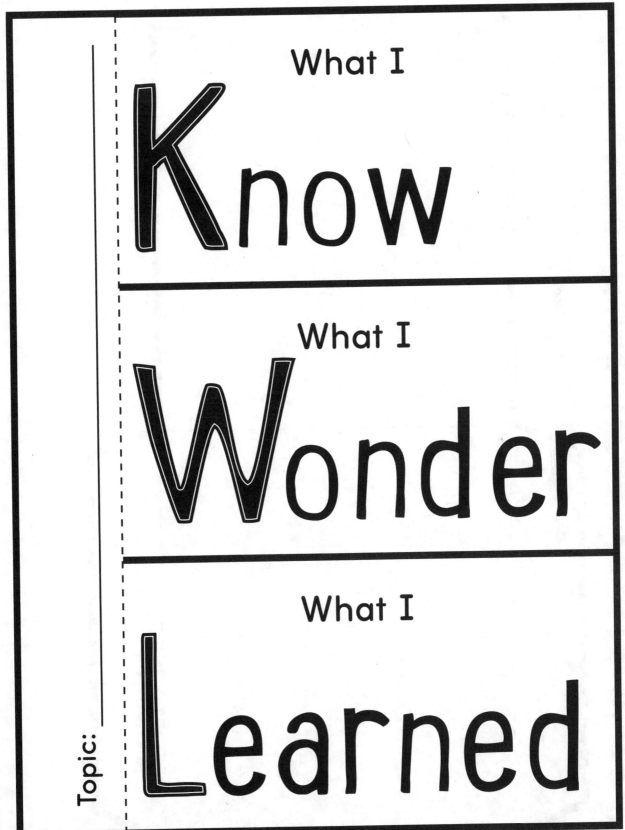

Library Pocket

Cut out the library pocket on the solid lines. Fold in the side tabs and apply glue to them before folding up the front of the pocket. Apply glue to the back of the pocket to attach it to a notebook page.

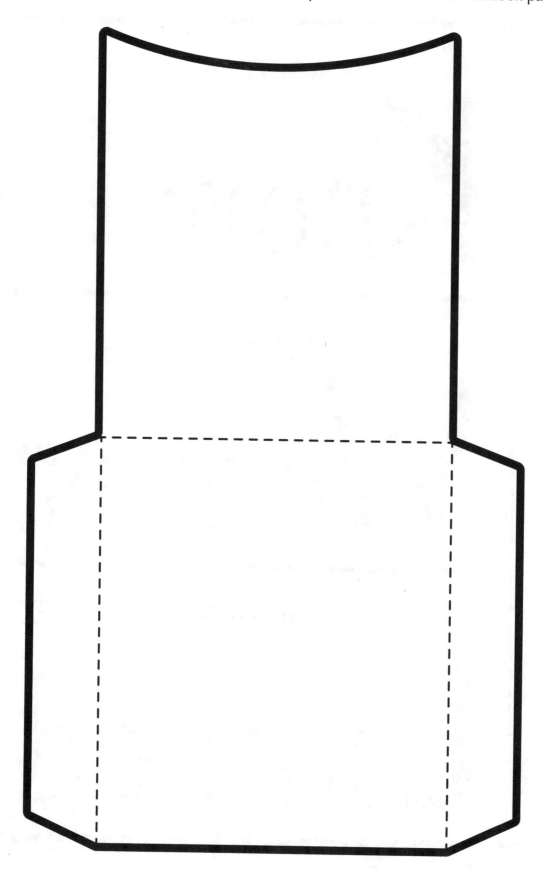

Envelope

Cut out the envelope on the solid lines. Fold in the side tabs and apply glue to them before folding up the rectangular front of the envelope. Fold down the triangular flap to close the envelope. Apply glue to the back of the envelope to attach it to a notebook page.

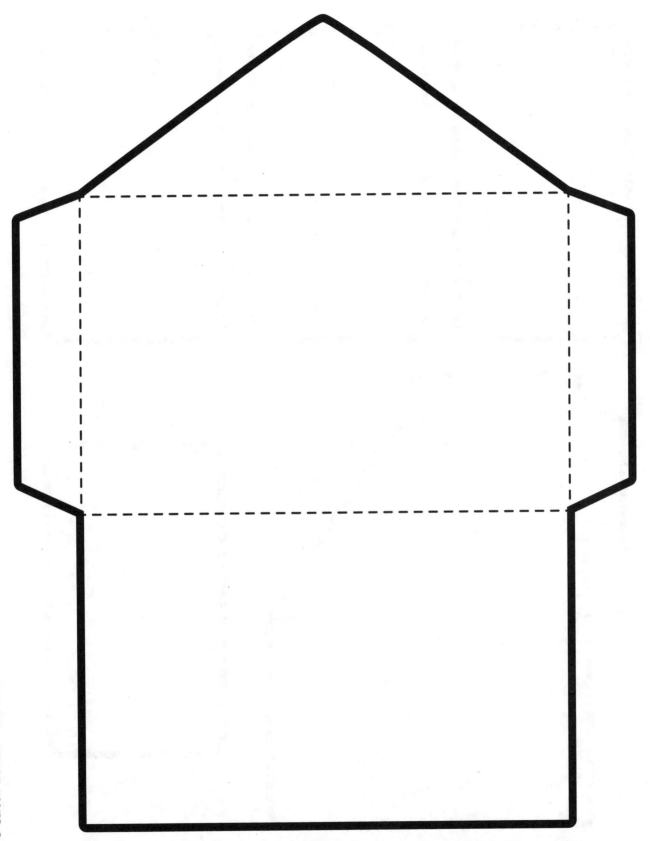

Pocket and Cards

Cut out the pocket on the solid lines. Fold over the front of the pocket. Then, apply glue to the tabs and fold them around the back of the pocket. Apply glue to the back of the pocket to attach it to a notebook page. Cut out the cards and store them in the envelope.

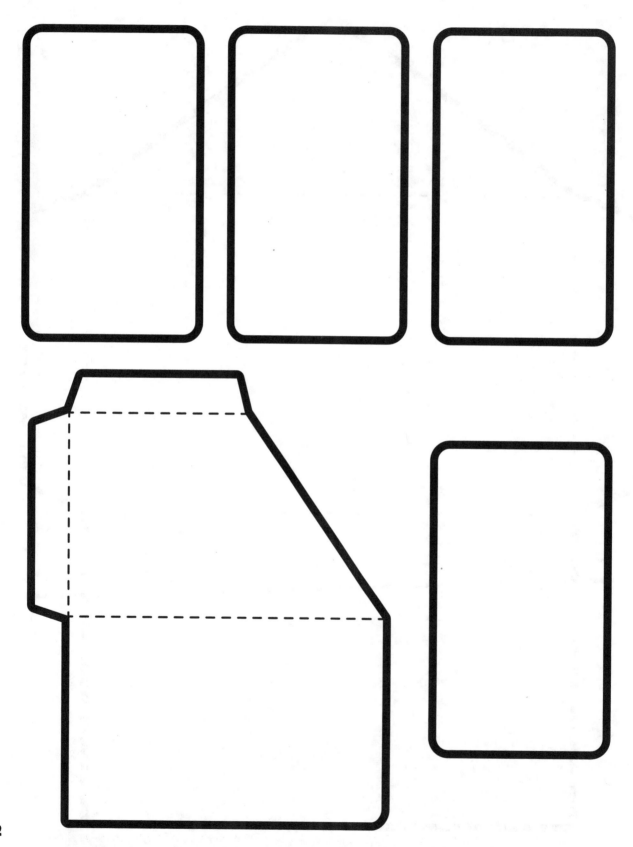

Six-Flap Shutter Fold

Cut out the shutter fold around the outside border. Then, cut on the solid lines to create six flaps. Fold the flaps toward the center. Apply glue to the back of the shutter fold to attach it to a notebook page.

If desired, this template can be modified to create a four-flap shutter fold by cutting off the bottom row. You can also create two three-flap books by cutting it in half down the center line.

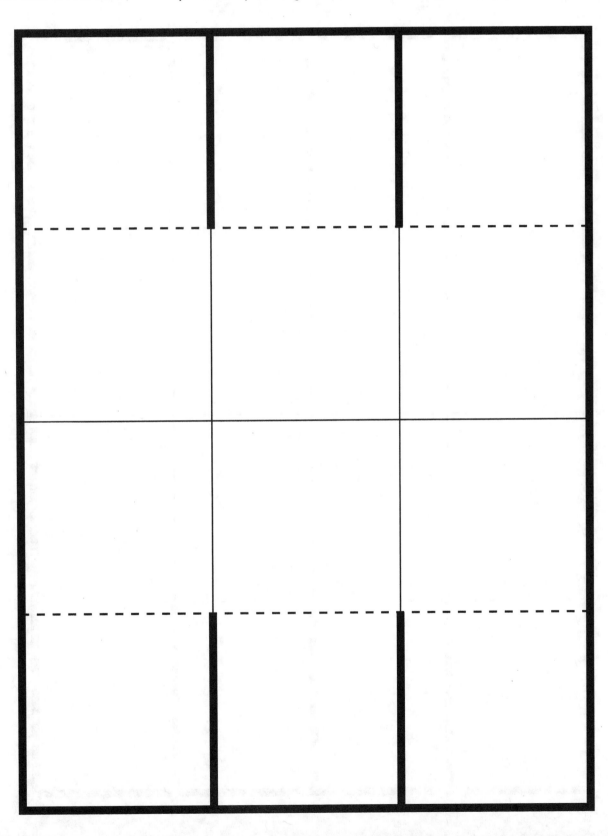

Eight-Flap Shutter Fold

Cut out the shutter fold around the outside border. Then, cut on the solid lines to create eight flaps. Fold the flaps toward the center. Apply glue to the back of the shutter fold to attach it to a notebook page.

If desired, this template can be modified to create two four-flap shutter folds by cutting off the bottom two rows. You can also create two four-flap books by cutting it in half down the center line.

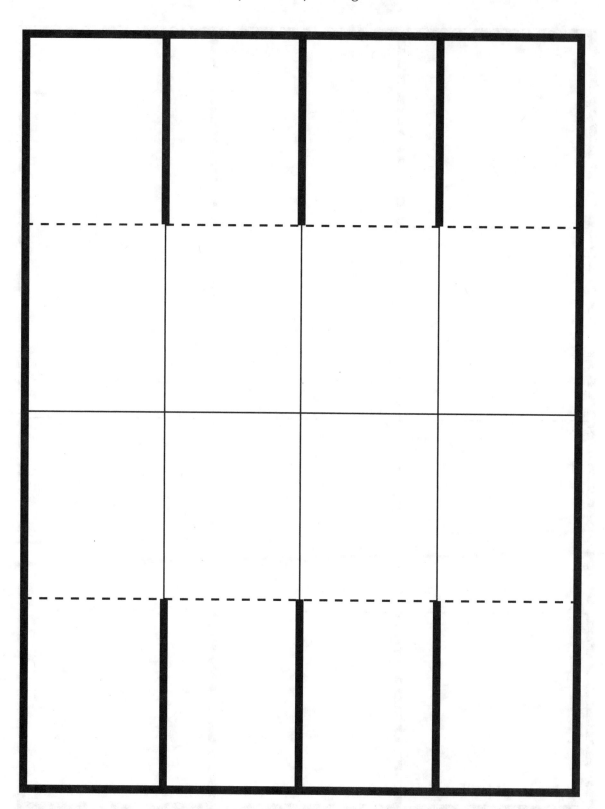

Flap Book—Eight Flaps

Cut out the flap book around the outside border. Then, cut on the solid lines to create eight flaps. Apply glue to the back of the center section to attach it to a notebook page.

If desired, this template can be modified to create a six-flap or two four-flap books by cutting off the bottom row or two. You can also create a tall four-flap book by cutting off the flaps on the left side.

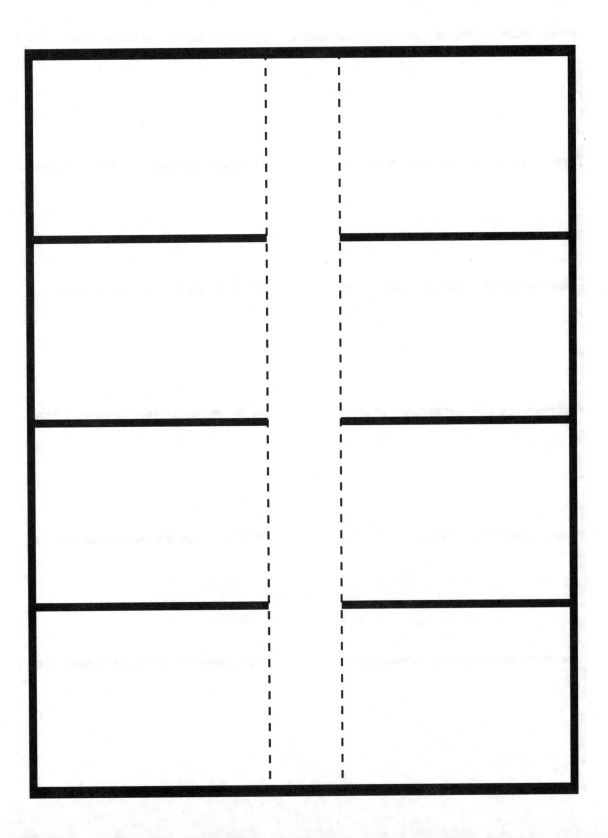

Flap Book—Twelve Flaps

Cut out the flap book around the outside border. Then, cut on the solid lines to create 12 flaps. Apply glue to the back of the center section to attach it to a notebook page.

If desired, this template can be modified to create smaller flap books by cutting off any number of rows from the bottom. You can also create a tall flap book by cutting off the flaps on the left side.

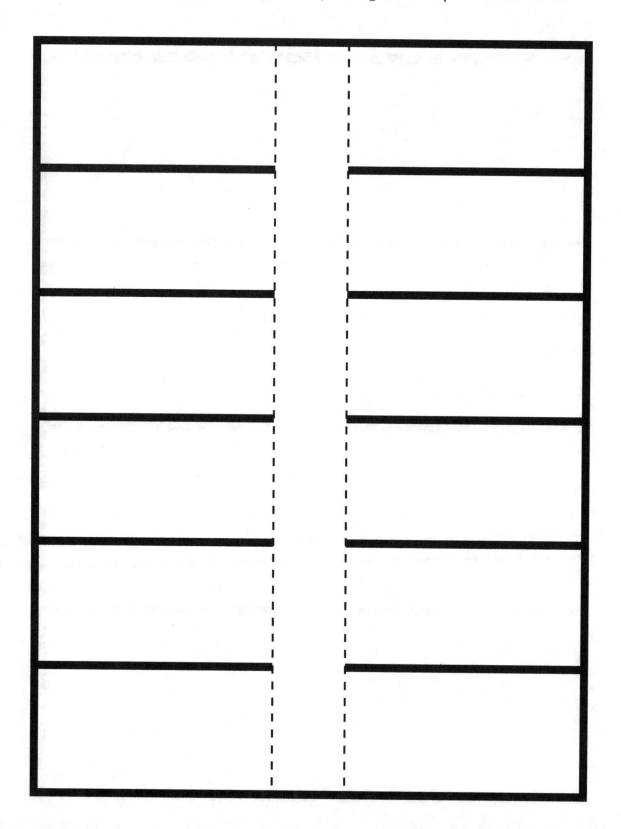

Shaped Flaps

Cut out each shaped flap. Apply glue to the back of the narrow section to attach it to a notebook page.

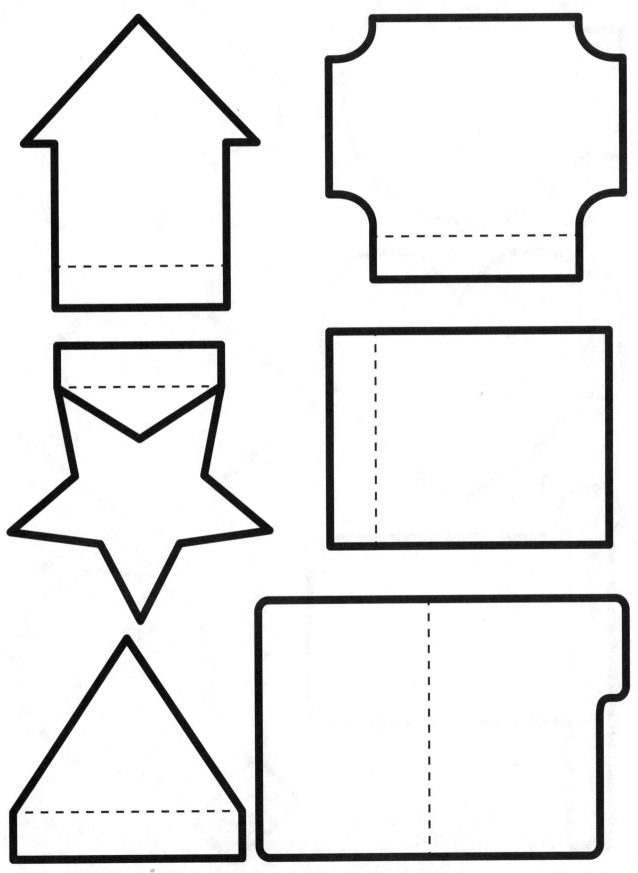

Shaped Flaps

Interlocking Booklet

Cut out the booklet on the solid lines, including the short vertical lines on the top and bottom flaps. Then, fold the top and bottom flaps toward the center, interlocking them using the small vertical cuts. Apply glue to the back of the center panel to attach it to a notebook page.

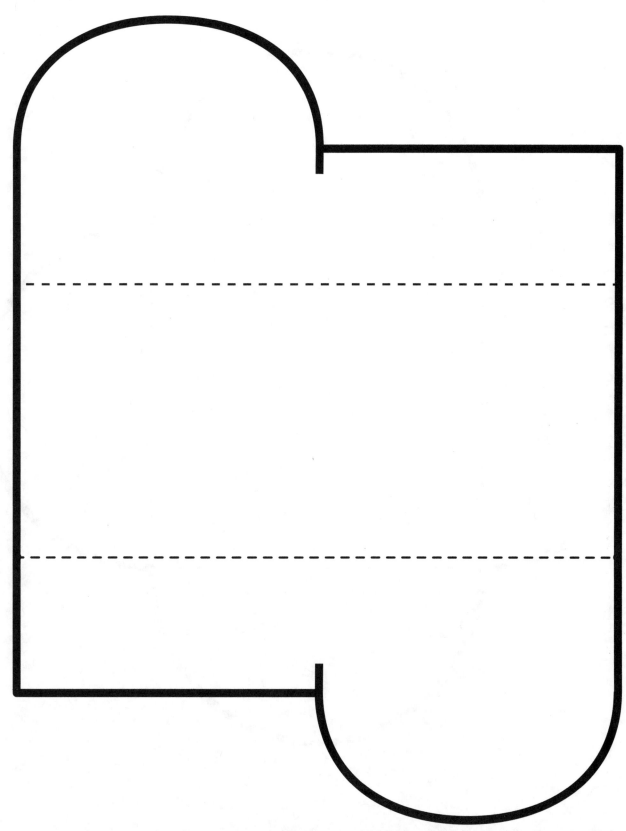

Four-Flap Petal Fold

Cut out the shape on the solid lines. Then, fold the flaps toward the center. Apply glue to the back of the center panel to attach it to a notebook page.

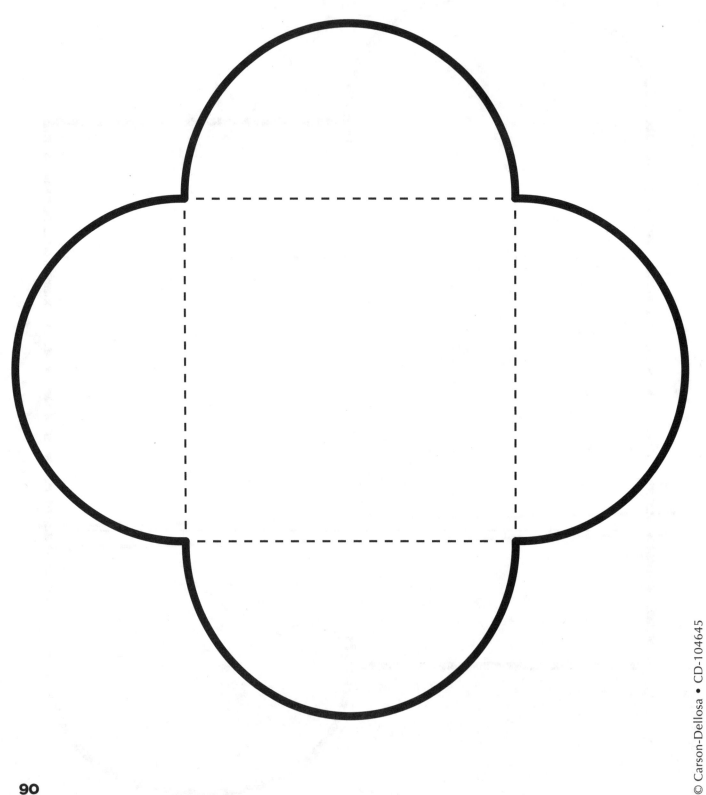

Six-Flap Petal Fold

Cut out the shape on the solid lines. Then, fold the flaps toward the center and back out. Apply glue to the back of the center panel to attach it to a notebook page.

Accordion Folds

Cut out the accordion pieces on the solid lines. Fold on the dashed lines, alternating the fold direction. Apply glue to the back of the last section to attach it to a notebook page.

You may modify the accordion books to have more or fewer pages by cutting off extra pages or by having students glue the first and last panels of two accordion books together.

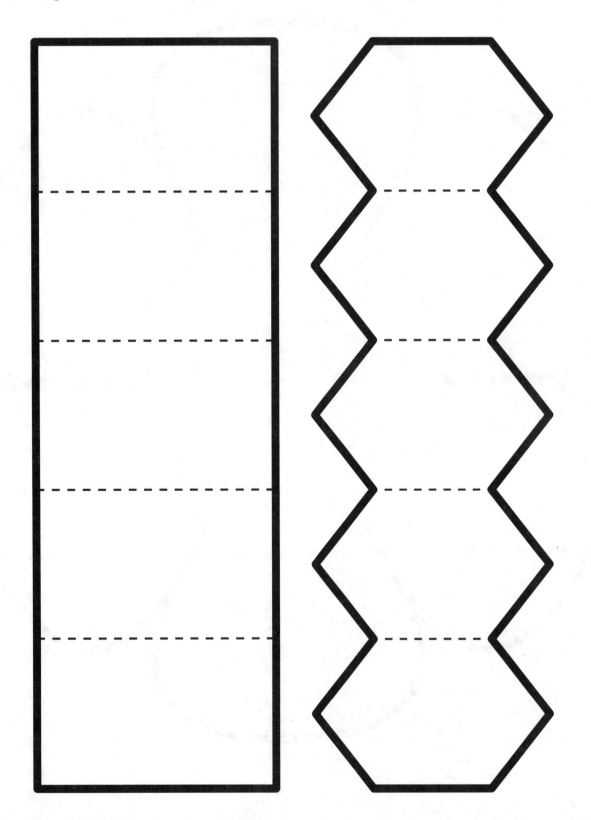

Accordion Folds

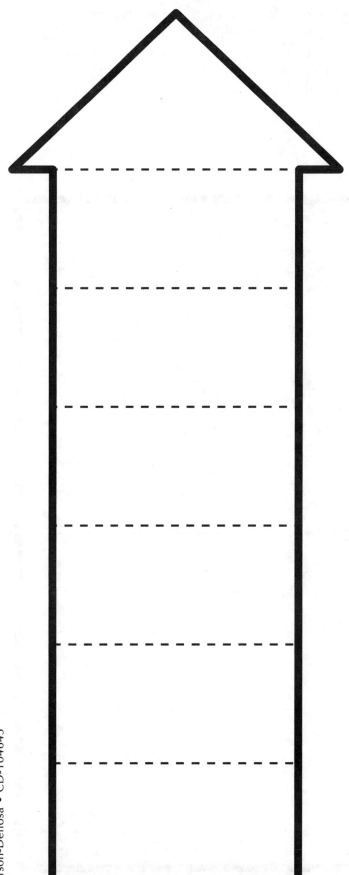

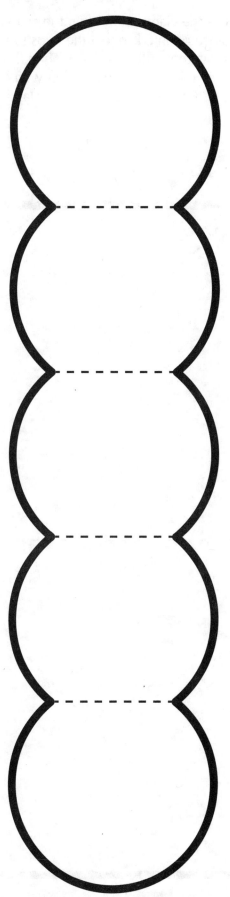

Clamshell Fold

Cut out the clamshell fold on the solid lines. Fold and unfold the piece on the three dashed lines. With the piece oriented so that the folds form an X with a horizontal line through it, pull the left and right sides together at the fold line. Then, keeping the sides touching, bring the top edge down to meet the bottom edge. You should be left with a triangular shape that unfolds into a square. Apply glue to the back of the triangle to attach the clamshell to a notebook page.

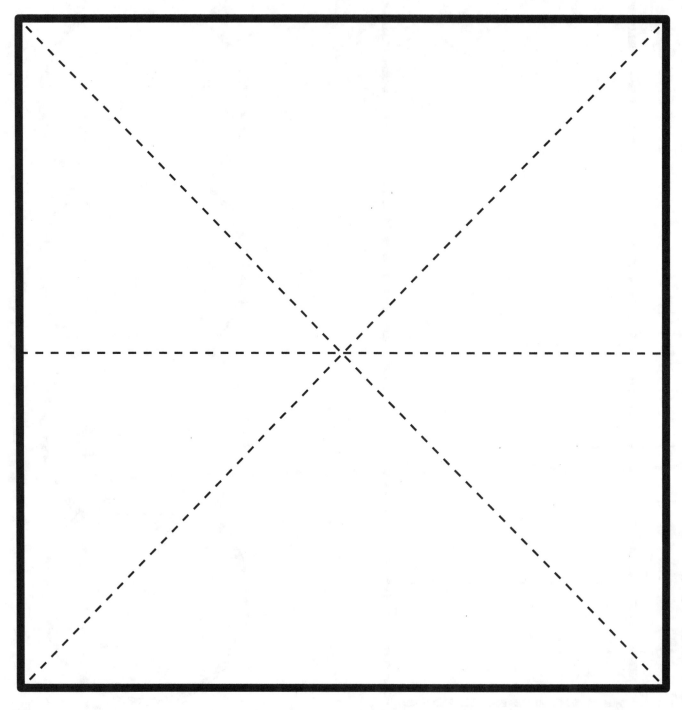

94

Puzzle Pieces

Cut out each puzzle along the solid lines to create a three- or four-piece puzzle. Apply glue to the back of each puzzle piece to attach it to a notebook page. Alternately, apply glue only to one edge of each piece to create flaps.

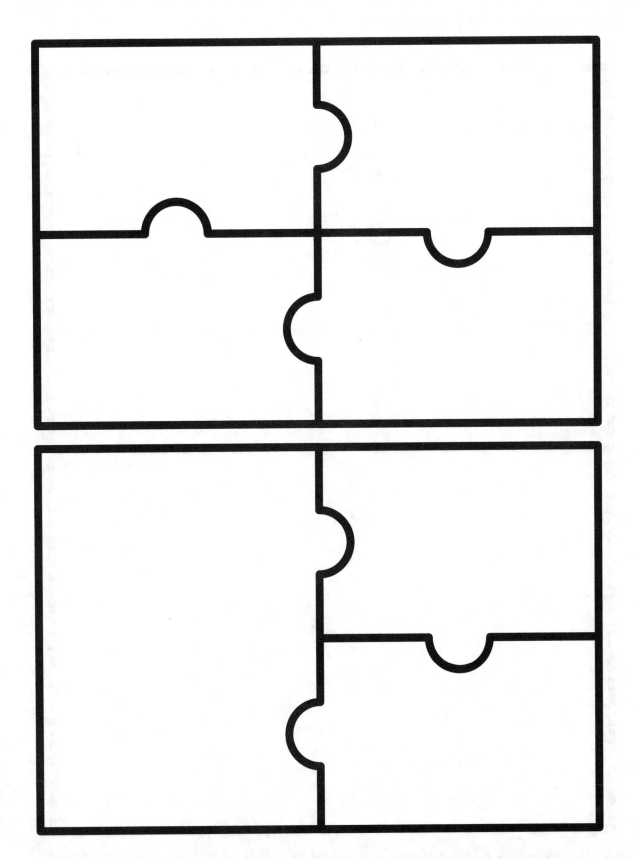

Flip Book

Cut out the two rectangular pieces on the solid lines. Fold each rectangle on the dashed lines. Fold the first piece so the gray glue section is inside the fold. Apply glue to the gray glue section and place the other folded rectangle on top so that the folds are nested and create a book with four cascading flaps. Make sure that the inside pages are facing up so that the edges of both pages are visible. Apply glue to the back of the book to attach it to a notebook page.

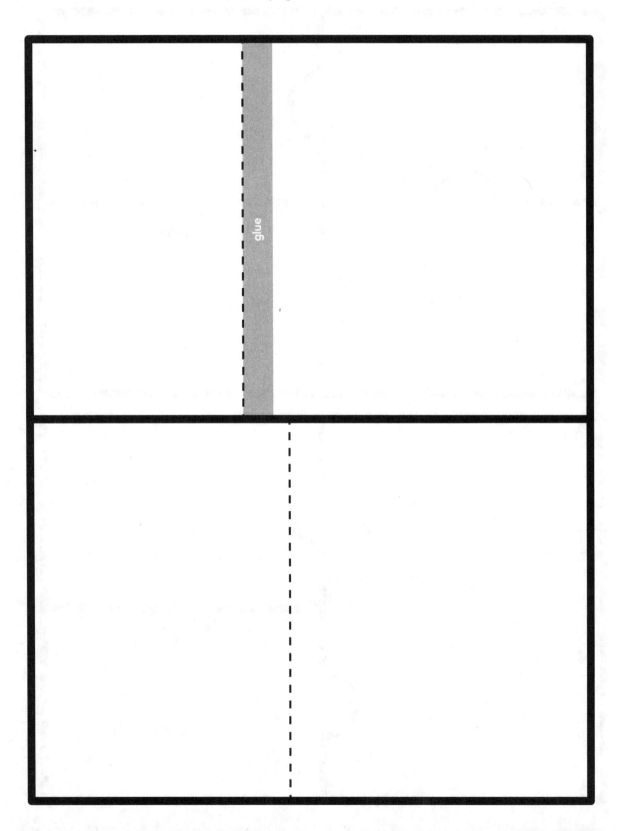

glue